Cedric Robinson
40 Years on Morecambe Bay

GREAT NORTHERN

GREAT NORTHERN BOOKS
Midland Chambers, 1 Wells Road, Ilkley, LS29 9JB

First published 2003
© Cedric Robinson 2003

ISBN: 0-9544002-2-4

By the same author
SAND PILOT OF MORECAMBE BAY
SAND WALKER

Printed by Amadeus Press Ltd, Bradford

Contents

Acknowledgements

A very special thank you to my wife Olive for her help and patience during the writing of this book, and to all of our family who gave support through a very worrying time during our daughter Diane's long illness. We should like to dedicate this book to Diane.

Special thanks to David Joy who gave me encouragement to write this book.

Personal thanks to Joan Heath who made an excellent job of typing the script from my scribble.

Many thanks to our son Paul who helped with the photographs. I am most grateful to everyone who provided photos and I am only sorry that it was not possible to use them all.

A lovely gesture and a welcome surprise was my 70th birthday cake baked by Anne Thistlethwaite of Elswick, Preston. It was iced and decorated by Mary Lowther of Over Wyresdale, Lancaster

Foreword
by Hunter Davies

One of the nicest, pleasantest, healthiest, happiest days in my whole life was walking across Morecambe Bay's sands with Cedric Robinson. I'm sure almost all of the 300,000 or so who have walked along with the Blessed Cedric since he was appointed a Queen's Guide in 1963 will have similar memories. And feel similarly grateful.

It was Cedric who resurrected the walk, gave it a public face, made it a regular event, free and open to everyone. He now conducts about 10,000 every year across the Sands, many of them on sponsored walks, a new and popular event in the last few years, which means that in so doing, he has also helped raise millions of pounds for charity.

I can't think of a better way of communing with nature than walking with Cedric, feeling part of the elements, in tune with sand and sea and sky and, on the horizon, the Lakeland landscape. It's something everyone should experience in their lives, because there is nothing quite like it anywhere else in Cumbria, in Britain, perhaps on the planet. There is a biblical feeling to it, of waters parting, dividing, sands receding.

The most natural element of all is Cedric himself, so humble, unassuming, so quiet. He has been showered with honourary degrees and awards, which is only right, but he remains the same, a natural, native son, who has never been abroad, never been in a plane, remaining part of the landscape he so clearly loves.

Many people who have walked with Cedric will also have noticed something else about him, something my wife immediately pointed out. He has the most beautiful feet. Let's hope they will be walking the Sands for many years to come.

Hunter Davies

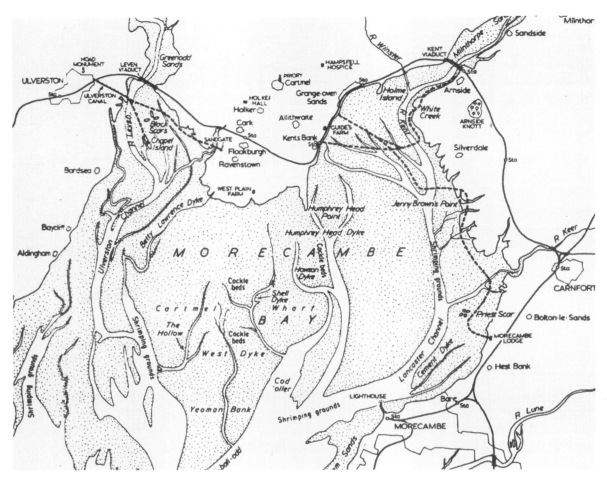

Morecambe Bay area and its fishing grounds. The routes of the cross-Bay walks, shown by dotted lines, vary according to local conditions. (Orginal drawing by Olive Robinson).

Introduction

How it all began

I started to follow the sands with my dad while still at school. They must have been in my blood, as my father, grandfather and even my grandmother all worked the sands for their livelihood. I could only go in school holidays and at weekends.

The most important job in the cold winter months was gathering cockles for the market towns of Lancashire and Yorkshire. Although cockles can be gathered all the year round, it was impossible to transport them during the summer as they would not keep as fresh as in the cool of winter. We did not have the luxury of refrigerators and freezers in those days! But whatever the weather, wind or rain or even fog, we would set out on the long journey into the Bay to fulfil our orders and try to make a living.

Our methods used were unique to the area and very unusual to people from elsewhere. Fishing is usually done from a boat but that is not possible from Flookburgh. The tide goes out for many miles, leaving sandbanks high and dry, with dykes and gullies which have been given names by the fishermen over the years. These drain down the sands back to the main rivers, which are the Kent and the Leven. We used horses and carts to take us out, so as well as learning about the sands from my father I also had to be able to look after the horse. Our lives depended upon a good and reliable horse!

As time moved on Flookburgh became a different village to the one I knew as a lad. One thing that stands out in my mind about those earlier days is the way the villagers spoke to one another - always in the local dialect. Going to school was a sore point for me because I did not enjoy it one little bit, but I must have done something right because I believe I was quite a good scholar. However, the call of the sands was never far away from my thoughts.

Flookburgh had a small community of people from all walks of life and the fishing families probably numbered around twenty or so. The fisherfolk were never closely knit, as most families over the years seemed to have their grievances regarding the sands. Yet our own family was very close, with my two sisters Peggy and Jean, my parents, one terrier dog called 'Crackers' and a cat which I had for twenty years.

A really big blow hit us when my father received his calling-up papers for World War 2. This took him away from us for five years and I often wonder how my mother managed. There was no running water or electricity in the house where we lived and I was born - No. 4 Market Cross in a row of six cottages opposite the public house called 'The Hope and Anchor'.

The war had started and my sisters and I were still attending school. The village had a new policeman. The previous one was well liked by the local community but all the villagers feared this younger one. Every household had to black out the windows so that no flicker of light could be seen. This policeman was nicknamed 'Blackout Joe' by the villagers because he was always on the prowl. Woe betide those found without proper blackout - he was onto them like a ton of bricks.

He frightened the life out of my mother one day as she saw him coming to the front door of the cottage. Unfortunately we were so poor that mother could not afford to renew our dog licence, so before opening the door to him she told me to take our terrier dog quickly out of the back door, thinking he would not know about it. Too late! He immediately said to mother that we had a dog with no licence and we would have to pay a fine. 'Blackout Joe' was a heartless soul because to pay the fine mother had to take in washing. As we had no electricity, the water had to be heated on the open fire and the dolly tub and posser used. These hard times always remain in your memories but we managed because we had such good neighbours who were kind and friendly.

After five long years dad returned from the Army safe and sound, so we were able to start fishing in the Bay for a living once again. Following the sands is a dangerous occupation and even with a lifetime's experience one is never too old to learn. One gets used to living with these dangers and over the years tends to get wiser. A well-known saying is 'a little knowledge is a dangerous thing'. However, when someone has a lifetime's experience on the sands and is a steady and level-headed person who can be trusted and followed, one can say that 'knowledge dispels fear'.

I was still a very young lad, but eager to learn and start fishing alongside my father with my very own horse and cart. In 1947 I left school behind at the age of fourteen and never felt happier. Most of my school pals left to go into a trade such as joinery, building or plumbing but I just wanted to follow the sands. In the winter months I went with my father gathering the cockles and had to work really hard to keep warm out on the sands, but as spring arrived and the weather improved with the days growing lighter we would each take a horse and cart.

Dad would stop off at the cockle beds about three or four miles out in the heart of the Bay and I would continue another mile or so down to the shrimping grounds. When dad was asked how his lad was doing at fishing he replied that he was shaping well. He admits that he was always a bit worried about me shrimping down the Bay on my own and felt a sigh of relief when he spotted me on the horizon, coming up from the lower grounds to meet up with him once again.

I just loved going onto the sands and felt that I never wanted to leave them, but at the age of eighteen I was called up into the Army for two years' National Service. Apart from visiting Morecambe and Blackpool I had never been away from the village before, but now I had to report to Blandford in Dorset where I did my training. That was where, along with others, I was made to feel about two feet tall or should I say small! We were bawled at from dawn till dusk and could not do right for doing wrong. I am sure everyone in our squad did his best but it was not good enough. If you failed to salute an officer - and there were many of them - you were bawled at again. So to get it right we would salute anything that moved, sometimes getting it wrong and made to feel such an idiot.

It did become more tolerable when the weeks of training were finally over and I was posted to a much smaller army camp at Sedgefield in County Durham. After twelve months I was moved to Fulwood Barracks at Preston where I was able to travel home at weekends now and again. I could then visit the local dances, which I always enjoyed. They were held at the Rink in Barrow-in-Furness, the Coronation Hall at Ulverston, or the Pier, the Winter Gardens or the Floral Hall in Morecambe. I was called upon to do fishing out in the Bay many times in the early hours after these enjoyable late nights out with my mates. But I could not wait for those two very long years to end and get back to my family and friends.

In spring 1960 I met Olive who was a widow with four young children. Bill was the eldest aged 13 years, then Robert, Diane and Paul. I asked Bill if he would like to earn some money by coming to help me with the market gardening as we had two smallholdings. He was a very good and willing help, gathering vegetables and packing them into the van ready for an early start to the market at Barrow-in-Furness on Wednesdays, Fridays and Saturdays. Mum and dad had a stall there where they would sell our home-grown vegetables and also the flukes, shrimps and cockles caught out in the Bay by Bill and me.

This was the beginning of a lasting friendship with Olive and her family as we came to know each other very well. We married at St John the Baptist Church in Flookburgh on October 30th, 1961. I then moved into the house in Ravenstown where Olive had lived with her family. On 3rd January 1963 our daughter Jean was born and this added to our happiness.

Bill came out onto the sands with me regularly now as he had left school. One day, while out cockling miles from the shore, the North Western Sea Fisheries Officer, Gren Harrison, appeared as if from nowhere. He was the law officer of the sands and occasionally he would turn up and inspect the size of the cockles we were gathering. A well-built chap and very strong, he always wore a uniform similar to that of a naval officer and thigh boots that must have been a drag when walking all that way across the sands. I always thought him to be very fair with the local fishermen, as some of them did not always tow the line - and I always seemed to get on well with him.

On this occasion Bill and I were about to make ready for home when he offered to help load the cockles onto the cart. The bags weighed all of a hundredweight but he loaded all the cockles by himself without even taking down the cart's tailboard (known locally as the 'cart eck'). He just simply lifted them clean over and into the bottom of the cart without any effort at all. As we moved away from the cockle grounds making for home, Gren walked alongside the horse and cart chatting away. Then he happened to mention that the Guide over the sands at Grange, Mr Burrow, was retiring and he thought I would be a likely candidate for the job.

Sand Pilot

The Official Guide across the sands
Is appointed by the Queen
To guide the weary traveller
across the sands so mean
The history of the post
goes back for many a year
To lead all those who travelled
across the Leven, Kent and Keer
The guide would walk the sands
and fish out in the bay
To get to know the dangerous parts
and find the safest way
He has to do this every day
because the bay is fickle
The rivers can change into a torrent
where yesterday there was a trickle
The mud itself is mobile
Sandbanks move around the bay
He has to know it inside out
and where the quicksand lay
Many a coach and traveller
have tried it on their own
In Cartmel Priory Churchyard
you'll find their names upon a stone
So when you take a short cut
to avoid the longest way
Make sure you're on the Oversands Route
with the Sand Pilot of Morecambe Bay

Lynn Wilman (1998)

Gren talked freely about it and said that if I was at all interested I would have to apply in writing and he would give me the address. When Bill and I got home from the sands, the cockles were unloaded and the horse put in the stable down Moor Lane with a feed and off home we went. Olive had a meal ready for us, as out there on the sands always seemed to give us a good appetite. I told her what Gren had said about the Guide's job becoming available at Grange. She was quite happy living in Ravenstown but would go along with whatever I should decide. I applied in writing and was asked to go for an interview before finally being chosen as the 'Queen's Guide to the Kent Sands of Morecambe Bay' later in 1963.

In the meantime Olive's parents had come from Leeds to stay with us for a week's holiday. Her mother asked where were we going to live. Olive had never been to Cart Lane before so her mother suggested that they went along just to have a look at the place. They set off from Ravenstown and walked to Flookburgh Square with baby Jean in the pushchair. As they waited at the bus stop along came the bus for Grange. They took their seats not knowing where to get off, so the conductor put them off at Cardrona and kindly gave them directions to Cart Lane. Olive did not want to appear nosy as that is not her nature, but thought it would be nice to see the place and show her mother where we would be living.

Carter Road was downhill so Olive kept a tight hold of the pushchair with baby Jean strapped safely inside. This was a good precaution as this is a steep hill of about 1 in 4. They could see buildings at the lower end of the fields, close to the railway line, so at the bottom of Carter Road near the railway cottage and crossings they turned right and within a short distance came across the house - Guide's Farm.

There was a man standing just outside the front door. It was the Guide, Mr Burrow, but Olive had not met him before so she asked, 'Please can you tell me if this is Guide's Farm?' and he replied 'Yes' quite cheerfully. He said that he was Mr. Burrow and asked if Olive was my wife. 'My missis is down Grange doing a bit of shopping so I can't show you round. We're not quite ready for moving as we've some apples to pick up in yon orchard' - which he pointed out. 'And that's about it,' he said.

We eventually moved to Guide's Farm, Grange, in early October 1963 and that is how it all began.

1. Across the Bay
The First Walk

After settling into our new home, we were kept very busy during the winter months decorating and painting as well as going out onto the sands cockling. That winter was an extremely cold one and we did not have any heating that was adequate - no electricity, just the coal fire in an open grate in the large living room. When we got up in the morning the flannel in the bathroom was sometimes frozen to the sink. That does not happen any more because we now have calor-gas heaters but still no central heating. If you are brought up to live without these kind of things when you are young, I am sure you become hardier and can put up with conditions that a younger generation would probably not tolerate today.

As soon as spring came along the first walk took place in April 1964. Guide's Farm had no telephone when we moved in so we had to rely on letters coming from interested parties. I had already received confirmation of who I was to lead across the Bay. There were thirteen paratroopers on a military exercise on a day that weather-wise could not have been worse. Bitterly cold and heavy showers was the menu for the day, so my son Bill and I decided to wear our fishing gear and that meant oilskins and waders.

The crossing was from Hest Bank near Morecambe to Grange-over-Sands, which was a distance of about nine miles. The River Keer, which runs out into the Bay from Carnforth, is much smaller than the Kent but can be difficult to cross, especially if there has previously been heavy rainfall. Luckily, we did not encounter any problems and walked on without looking back. We now set our line of journey for Jenny Brown's Point and in the distance beyond was the village of Silverdale. We made good time and being a small group of fit young men did not have to make any stops. Before long the wide River Kent could be seen in the distance. As we approached you would have thought that in no way could we wade through the huge expanse of moving water but we did! A wide river is a much better and safer crossing than a narrow one.

With the fast flow our small party kept close together until the point where it began to get shallower, then the pace quickened. We crossed safely through the river onto the Grange shore. The worst part of this crossing was the last hundred yards or so coming up the muddy shore near the bathing pool on the promenade, where we could hardly lift our feet from the suction of the sand. The officer in charge of the platoon said that the conditions on the day were ideal for his soldiers to have experienced, but this was one experience Bill and I wanted to forget!

How the walk began

The next walk - again from Hest Bank to Grange-over-Sands - took place in the middle of May and the weather had really warmed up for this one. It was a perfect day. I had travelled round to the other side by train from Kents Bank station to Carnforth, from where I managed to catch a bus to Hest Bank without much of a wait. This group comprised about twenty men and women ramblers.

The day was bright and visibility clear and Olive had seen us coming away in the distance through my powerful binoculars. She is very thoughtful and caring and had prepared a nice tea for us. Olive asked our daughter Diane to come to the crossing gates at Cart Lane with the message that she was expecting us to go along to the farm. We all trudged along the lane, Olive greeting us at the door with a smile and inviting everyone inside for tea. After taking off our shoes and leaving them and our haversacks in a tidy heap on the floor, we filed in and almost filled the living and sitting rooms. Olive had already made the sandwiches so she told us she would only be a minute brewing the tea.

Several of the walkers were by now desperate for the toilet so that took a bit of time, but then we all managed to find a seat somewhere to sit down and relax. All was quiet at first but then one after another they started to ask questions that were mainly about the old house and its history. Tea was brewed and Diane came round with the sandwiches, and then Olive appeared from the kitchen carrying one of those very large aluminium teapots. You will probably have seen them some time as they were used at wedding receptions, village hall parties, Women's Institute meetings and even at funerals. They are very heavy when full and have a handle at each side so that you can hold them steady and pour without spilling.

On this occasion our teapot came in very handy with these thirsty walkers and we had a really good time. They thanked us over and over again for our hospitality. Olive thought that this was the normal thing to do but as time went on the numbers of enquiries grew and grew into hundreds and more hundreds so now there is no way I could invite the walkers back to Guide's Farm for tea!

I never knew how Olive came to have that large aluminium teapot, but I do remember that our good neighbours in Cart Lane used to come and borrow it when they were having a family party or some other special occasion. One of our neighbours sadly borrowed it when her husband died. Olive and I were invited back to the house after the funeral along with the old teapot, which we still have.

I jotted down details of another walk in the 1960s in a notebook: "A nasty wet day, party left Hest Bank near Morecambe at 1.45 pm. The first obstacle was the River Keer. Found this very soft with the heavy rainfall, and was difficult to ford. Stopped the group halfway across the Bay on a high sandbank about two miles out from the village of Silverdale. After twenty minutes we set off for Grange crossing the River Kent between Blackstone Point and Holme Island, that being the only suitable place to cross. The river knee deep and a good crossing. We came ashore at the bathing pool at Grange-over-Sands on the promenade.

Party consisted of 26 from Blackburn Technical College, 40 from Ripon in Yorkshire, others from Wakefield, Lancaster and Preston. One hundred and fifty walkers in all, and this was the first walk of the season."

The walk, once an annual event, was now about

to change. I would soon be organising about twelve walks a year and they seemed to catch on in a big way. A shorter working week was attributed to more walks taking place. People could arrange to come on either a Saturday or a Sunday and this was how it started to grow. The greater demand meant a lot of organisation for me to arrange each walk - the date, time, place to start and to finish, and checking each crossing beforehand.

High tide weekends are unsuitable so I have to plan for the neaps. Each season varies with the number of dates I can choose for a walk, but with the demand being as great as it is, I am now able to choose around thirty possible weekend dates and also a number of midweek ones. We are now encountering climate changes with milder winters and much milder and warmer springs. With these changes I find I can now organise and start the walks in April and continue right through the summer until the end of September. The Tourist Board Information Centre is now taking a wide

interest with many enquiries regarding the dates and times of the walks and the public are travelling very long distances to take part in them.

Today, walking is a national hobby that is encouraged to help people keep fitter, healthier and live longer. The Morecambe Bay Walk fits that bill because people of all age groups and from all walks of life can take part and really enjoy the same experience - 'getting away from it all'! There are not many places in the world today where you can leave it all behind but Morecambe Bay with its peace and tranquillity is one of them.

The walk is now known internationally and enquiries come from afar. Whatever the weather on the day, people still genuinely enjoy the 'walk with a difference'. Although some of them are tired at the end, it is so rewarding that they always say how much they have enjoyed this unique and wonderful experience and ask to come again.

Sponsored Walks

A key factor that has contributed to the ever-increasing popularity of the cross-Bay walk is its success as a means of fund-raising, with some groups now numbering in excess of five hundred. One of the most consistently successful is Galloway's Society for the Blind, which in its first sponsored walk with just 100 participants raised what was then considered 'a fantastic £7,000'. It has since gone on to raise over £100,000 in eleven years in what has become its most successful regular event.

Here is just a selection of charities that have benefited from sponsored walks across the Bay. Except where otherwise stated the amounts relate to a single crossing:

Barnardos (Milnthorpe):
£9,402 by 562 people in 1992.
Bolton Hospice:
'An amazing £9,144' in 2002.
British Heart Foundation:
Around £15,000 over three years.
Cath's Fund of Friendship (for leukemia sufferers): *'A phenomenal £10,000' in 1996.*
Christie's against Cancer (Altrincham & Sale):
Just over £13,000 by 100+ walkers.
Cystic Fibrosis Trust (North West Region):
£6,500.

Derian's House Children's Hospice:
More than £25,000.
Hospice Care for Burnley & Pendle:
£7,500 in 2002.
Liver Cancer Appeal, Liverpool:
£15,500 in 2000; £10,000 in 2001.
Parkinson's Disease Society:
Over £7,000 in October 1999.
Rainbow Family Trust (Francis House children's hospice, Manchester): *£3,000.*
Royal National Institute for the Blind (Lancashire): *£12,000 in May 2002.*
Sight Savers International:
In excess of £18,000 from a series of annual walks.
Sue Ryder Care: *£50,000.*

Some of the letters I have received have been extremely touching. One that I shall always remember came from Kevin Lonegan of Galloway's: 'We are truly indebted to you Cedric. If it wasn't for you giving up your time and expertise none of the thousands upon thousands of people would have had the experience of a lifetime, enjoying one of the country's most popular days out. Without you none of the many, many charities you have supported would have benefited and you must be indirectly responsible for helping to raise hundreds of thousands of pounds.'

The Changing Sands

The most dramatic tidal situation in Britain occurs in Morecambe Bay, where the sea recedes for many miles twice a day. Changes are taking place the whole of the time, but the most striking can be seen following high tides, strong winds and heavy rainfall. All of these contribute to movements of sand from one area to another. What has been a safe route to take one day can be quite the opposite on the following day - soft and dangerous and so beguilingly innocent. Yes, peaceful appearances are deceptive, because when the tide is out water drains away unevenly below the surface of the sand, leaving some parts firm but others deadly quicksand.

The speed of the tide has a powerful influence on all these changes as it makes its way up the Bay like a galloping horse, constantly reshaping channels, dykes and dangerous gullies. No accurate map of the Bay with its river channels could ever be drawn because of these constant changes. There is a large tidal range of 10 metres and during the neaps and low water tides there are over 100 square miles of drying foreshore.

The action of high tides and winds contributes to erosion around our coasts but deposits on the shore are mainly due to sediment brought down the rivers and secondly to eroded material from adjoining coasts. Sand is moved up an estuary by wave action and the strong flood tides and then dropped on the higher banks. The balance can only be maintained by erosion on the ebb from constantly moving channels and dykes. However, in the upper reaches of Morecambe Bay away from the main rivers, the Kent and Leven, the ebb tide does not have the power to distribute the sand over the width of the estuary. So there it stays, and continues to build up until the main river moves back into that area.

The Kent estuary has also undergone change due to man's activities, which have combined to produce adverse as well as beneficial effects over the years. In 1851 a Lancaster businessman, William Stout, referred in his autobiography to the Kent running close into the shore at Silverdale with a drop of ten feet or more into the bed of the river. Later in the 1850s the construction of the Furness Railway was a great achievement and also a formidable undertaking with ten miles of sea embankments and viaducts over the Kent and Leven each about 500 yards long. The railway was to transform Grange into an attractive holiday resort but the biggest change in the ebb and flow of the tides in Morecambe Bay was about to begin. The River Kent moved close to the Grange shore and there it remained for a long period.

Following my appointment as Guide, the main route for the Bay walks started from the Hest Bank shore just over the railway crossing and at the Grange side came onto the shore by the railway station or on the promenade adjacent to the swimming pool. You could almost set your clock on the time it took to cross - no more than three hours - as this formed a direct route for those early crossings. Jenny Brown's Point was reckoned to be our halfway marker after walking for one and a half hours. With the river being away from Silverdale, Carnforth and Bolton-le-Sands, the sandbanks were usually high and dry and this was our ideal place to stop and have a break. We must have been at least two miles off shore, well out into the Bay from Silverdale.

Then came the winter months of 1982-3 with high tides and north-westerly gales that caused havoc around our coastline and played a great part in bringing about the changes we have witnessed during the past twenty years. The River Kent changed almost overnight, leaving the Grange shore and moving over to the Silverdale and Carnforth marshes. This altered the whole outlook of the Bay.

The spring of 1983 was the wettest on record and, after the long winter of high tides backed by gales, I knew there were bound to be changes. Yet nothing had prepared me for what I found when I did a recce for my first walk of the season on 6th May. It had rained all the previous day and, although it was now fine for the first time, visibility was poor with hazy conditions and the air was very humid. All landmarks were blotted from view but the sun was trying to break through the haze. I could just make out the rocky outcrops of Priest Skear at Hest Bank but on the approach could hardly anticipate what was ahead of me.

I soon realised that the Kent had moved dramatically away from the Grange side of the Bay and was now getting a hold of Priest Skear. To come across changes so great can be a little scary at the time. The river was at its peak in full spate from the previous rainfall and was like a roaring sea.

The best thing to do was to go up alongside the River Keer. My son-in-law Chris was with me on this expedition - or should I say 'adventure' - and we were still close to the shore as we could vaguely see the outline through the haze. The Kent channel had eaten its way towards the Silverdale side of the Bay and really taken hold of the marsh. Every now and again we would hear the sound of huge chunks of sand being toppled into the bed of the river due to the fast flow.

Visibility was still only a matter of yards and the whole situation was becoming very eerie. The outlet of the Keer had been shortened and the river was much reduced in distance before it met up with the Kent. The slagheaps at Carnforth were now only a stone's throw from where Chris and I stood, but the Kent had sliced acres from the marshland and there was a drop into the riverbed of at least ten feet. We had to take a very different route from that planned when we had set out.

According to what I have read, these changes occur in cycles of seventy to one hundred years. If this is true, we have a long time to wait for the River Kent to make a change for the better and once again run along the shore at Grange and Kents Bank.

In the meantime, Grange Town Council is concerned about the retaining wall where the River Winster enters the estuary. It claims it is preventing the Kent channel taking a course towards the promenade at Grange. This has led to silting up, the invasion of unsightly spartina grass and surface water drainage problems in the lower lying parts of the town.

Route changes

The sudden change in the course of the River Kent meant that the Morecambe Bay Walk had to take a different route as it neared Jenny Brown's Point. What had for years been high and stable ground now looked almost impassable. This meant that I had to keep nearer to the land than previously as the drain-offs from the marsh at the Point were in places hollow and very soft.

We continued this route for a while until erosion at the Silverdale side of the Bay was so great that the only alternative left was to take to the road at the Point. We then walked along to Silverdale village and took to the shore again where there is a small row of cottages. We had to continue following the shore past Cove Lane until we came to Park Point, where after all that time we were able to walk out onto the sands and cross the Kent on our way over to Kents Bank. This walk took about 5 hours and 30 minutes. It was so boring and took far too long as well as having to leave the sands for a surfaced road, but I found a safe alternative route starting from Silverdale that I used for about four years.

(Opposite top) Heading across the Bay on an early walk, with Cedric Robinson and Olive striding out on the left. (Axcil Poignent).

(Opposite lower) The first walk of the 1964 season was also the first to be led by Cedric following his appointment as 'Queen's Guide to the Kent Sands of Morecambe Bay' in November 1963. Then only 30, he is seen on the right of the photograph.

The striking feature of both these pictures is the small numbers compared with present-day walks.

Although it was much shorter, walkers still came in large parties and enjoyed the experience just the same. The railway station at Silverdale is quite a way from the village but a footpath cuts down the distance considerably. I enjoyed the walks starting from Silverdale because I had one or two friends in the village on whom I could call if I had time to spare. The Burrow's family butcher, the late Dick Proctor, enjoyed testing the sands with me and he was such a knowledgeable character. Jeff Altham accompanied me on many a crossing. He and his late wife had a shop on the premises so I often called and was always offered a welcome cuppa.

Strong tides during the past four years had played havoc with the Silverdale coastline. Whereas the Kent was not too far away from the shore, it had again been moving rapidly, with rocks appearing that had been buried under the sands and marshland for over a hundred years. This move soon put an end to the walks starting from Silverdale, but luckily further up the Bay at Arnside and White Creek the river was now running favourably for a sands' crossing. The picturesque village of Arnside has become the people's choice for the start of the walk, although it is now once again possible to cross from Hest Bank.

A Typical Crossing

For almost twenty-five years I led the walks from Hest Bank and Morecambe Lodge Farm across the sands to Grange. Looking back at photographs and cine film, it was rare to find many children or senior citizens included in the groups making the crossing. The railway station at Hest Bank was closed so many of the walkers would arrange to travel to the start by coach. Only a few went by train to Carnforth, where it was sheer luck if you could find a bus connection to take you the rest of the journey to Hest Bank. I preferred to walk rather than wait for a bus, not knowing whether one would turn up or not, so I was walking the whole time.

In those first years following my appointment the walks were hardly known compared with today, so it was rare to have someone from afar. Now it is quite different, as they are known both nationally and internationally and also through the Internet. People travel long distances - and even all the way from America - just to take part in one or more of my walks.

As I write the River Kent crossing for the Hest Bank walk is not a good one and is running deep, although it may alter for the better. Enquiries for this walk are now much reduced, as the alternative crossing from Arnside - the 'people's choice' - is the same distance and is also more exciting and suitable for all age groups.

I still organise a few crossings from Hest Bank and Morecambe Lodge Farm. When I arrive to lead them, I am generally met with a motley crowd of all ages from seven to seventy. Almost everyone is carrying a rucksack and many of them are bare-footed. It is almost a biblical scene as we set out across the sands - I carry my staff in my hand, whistle around my neck and my trainers stuffed into my rucksack. Moses must have been grateful when the Red Sea divided for them to cross.

We are about to cross an expanse of sand and water measuring 120 square miles and some of the walkers are no doubt wondering how will I manage to keep track of them all in this vast wilderness. The first mile or so of the eight-mile crossing is a process of acclimatisation, or in other words getting used to the idea.

On these low tide weekends the ridges of sand plus the worm casts (and at these early stages there are millions of them) are hard on the feet if there is a warm dry spell. Youngsters on the walk seem to think that they are live worms on the surface and watch very carefully where they are putting their feet until I tell them differently!

Slowly the group strings out to a length of about quarter of a mile. Ahead the sands drop lower as we approach a shallow water crossing that feels warm underfoot, almost like warm water from the tap. This is what the youngsters in the group have been waiting for, and after asking permission to run on ahead, they race away and splash through the shallow water enjoying themselves to the full.

A walk does not just happen and a lot of preparation goes into each and every sands' crossing. Usually on the Friday, prior to the popular Saturday and Sunday walks, I and my nephew Kenny walk the route, marking out the safest path and river crossing to take. Laurel branches are used as markers and put well down into the sand. It is always amusing to watch the dogs on a walk as they gallop towards a laurel marker. A tentative sniff, a cock up of the leg and

(Opposite, top) Water is often barely up to the knees. This happy throng, photographed in 2002, were taking part in an annual walk organised in aid of Galloway's Society for the Blind, a Lancashire-based charity. Over £100,000 has been raised in the last eleven years. One of the participants recently wrote of Cedric:

'I feel it is because this larger-than-life character is yet so kind and approachable that he is loved by so many people, and admired by so many who have never pulled on a pair of hiking boots but who know all about his struggle against ill-health. As Max Miller used to say: "There'll never be another." (Paul Nickson)

(Opposite, lower) On other occasions - especially when crossing the Keer and Kent rivers - the water can be much deeper. The Arnside shoreline remained comfortingly visible in the background when this group waded in up to the thighs during a cross-Bay walk in the early 1980s. (Jonathen Becker)

(This page) Certificates are distributed at the finish of the walk so that participants can prove to family and friends that they did it - and survived! These three walkers, photographed in September 2002, were among several hundred whom had just completed a crossing. Held in aid of Hospice Care for Burnley & Pendle, it raised £7,507.

before long there is a queue of them! They probably think I have put them there for their benefit - but never mind - it gives the group a bit of a laugh.

Now as the walkers stride out they must feel the sense of freedom and adventure all in one. What else do they see out there? Well, there is beauty all around and ahead of us. In the distance are the Lake District fells and over to the right in the east are the far-off hills of Yorkshire and the flat-topped mountain of Ingleborough. Over to our left the West Coast runs down from Ulverston to Barrow and the islands of Furness. A square black blob on the horizon is the remains of the ancient Piel Castle off Walney Island and nearby Roa Island is where the Barrow lifeboat is launched into Morecambe Bay. Dotted on the northern shoreline is the pretty hometown of Grange-over-Sands.

Our first river crossing is the Keer, running out into the Bay from Carnforth, and although this is shallow during a dry spell it is prone to quicksands after heavy rain. I spread the group at the edge of the river and ask them to wait while I go on ahead to ensure that all is well. Satisfied with conditions, I blow my whistle for the group to follow and give them a wave beckoning them towards me. Splash, splash, splash! - the youngsters race towards me ahead of the rest of the group and are having the time of their lives. Up on much higher ground clear from the water's edge, I stop and wait for everyone to leave the river before moving on.

The views from this point on a clear day are absolutely outstanding. This is the moment when the group can stand and take in the breathtaking beauty of the Bay all around. Looking back we can see Hest Bank, Morecambe and Heysham, and beyond is the Lune Valley. The River Lune winds its way down through Lancaster and enters the Bay below Middleton Sands.

Ashton Memorial with its dome-shaped head towers majestically above Williamson Park, Lancaster. Dubbed 'the Taj-Mahal of the North', it was commissioned by Lancaster-born millionaire Lord Ashton for his family. From the upstairs gallery is one of the best views in the area with the Lakeland fells, the Isle of Man and Blackpool visible on a clear day.

Way ahead, to the left of Kents Bank and near to Allithwaite and Flookburgh, is Humphrey Head, the limestone headland called 'Boxhill of the North' because of its wide variety of flora. Jutting out into the Bay, the headland is about160 feet above sea level at its highest point. Local folk have always called it Humphrey Head Point and it was famous in the early twentieth century when people came along and drank from the famous 'holy well' of St Agnes.

This well is difficult to find now and, although it still runs freely, is hidden under trees. My father, who is ninety-nine years young, told me that most people from the surrounding villages used to collect the water and at one time it was sold at tuppence a cup by a fishing family who inhabited a cottage next to the well. When the house fell into disrepair - which was inevitable because it was built too near the encroaching tides - the water was dispensed from a small wooden hut. Water from the 'holy well' was also barrelled and taken to Heysham, from where it was marketed as a 'cure-all' for holidaymakers. Take my dad's advice and leave the 'well' well alone or an upset tummy is on the cards and you may not be able to get to the nearest toilet quickly enough!

To the right of Humphrey Head and above Kents Bank is Kirkhead with its highest point the Tower, from where the whole expanse of Morecambe Bay and beyond can be seen. During the Second World War the Tower was a lookout point for the 'Home Guard'. The Germans dropped a 500-pound bomb in a field opposite Kirkhead Farm but the Army managed to defuse it safely the next day. There are still hollows in the ground as a result of enemy bombs in this area.

Grange-over-Sands faces south and is sheltered by Hampsfell Hospice which is 700 feet above sea level. To the north-east are the Howgills, the Pennines and hills of the Yorkshire dales. It is all awe-inspiring to the walkers as most of them have never been before, but the highlight of the Morecambe Bay Walk still lies ahead.

After crossing several small dykes we arrive at the water's edge of the Kent. Today it is a wide expanse looking not so much like a river but a running sea! Not to worry as I have been across the previous day testing the depth and the firmness of the riverbed for the number of walkers. I also marked the safe route between branches of laurel. From the markers I can see that the river is now shallower - and this is reassuring to the group.

I line everyone up between the laurels and usually have a joke with them before crossing. Some, a little apprehensive at this wide stretch of water, soon gain confidence as I blow the whistle and take a forward position. My nephew Kenny keeps an eye on the right flank while my good friend Mike, built like an oak tree and as strong as an ox, is at the other end. We proceed slowly as I try my hardest to keep the group together.

If some are a little frightened, keeping close together gives them confidence and they start to enjoy the experience of a lifetime. Occasionally one or two people scream out, but not to worry as they are in no danger - they have trodden on a Morecambe Bay fluke. Some of the womenfolk almost jump out of their knickers as they suddenly stand on something slippery about the size of a dinner plate. As the water deepens the pace slows down but it quickens again as it becomes shallow towards the Grange side, with the children and dogs racing to be the first on the other side.

This crossing must certainly be a magical experience for everyone taking part. We stand for a while, people chat, make new friends and even decide to take a snack or a drink from their rucksacks as I wait till the last person is on firm sand clear of the river before moving on. There is no hurry at this stage and there are lots of things to see and questions to be asked.

Over to our right is the village of Silverdale and at this point we can see the Furness Railway embankment and the viaduct over the River Kent, although Arnside is hidden from view. With Kents Bank station now in sight the pace quickens, and although I can walk with the best of them this is not the right way to do it. I am responsible for everyone on the walk, especially those at the rear, so the whistle is blown and we all gather together, probably for the last time, before coming ashore at Kents Bank. After three hours we make our way over the marshy area and up onto terra firma.

Olive has come down with a friend by car and this is parked to meet us as we come in from a very enjoyable walk. A certificate and a copy of one of my books are available from the boot of the car, providing walkers with evidence to show their friends that they completed the trip safely. Afterwards they can settle down comfortably at home and read all about it! Not everyone stops at the car to meet up with Olive, as they are in too much of a hurry to get to the nearest toilets, but they miss out on a treat. However, many do spare the time to have a chat and some ask for me to join them for a photograph before eventually returning home by car or coach.

The 'people's choice'

As already mentioned, a more exciting walk now starts from the lovely seaside village of Arnside. The meeting place for the start of the 'people's choice' is Ash Meadow, which is at the end of the promenade and the beginning of the public footpath along the shore. Walkers taking this route keep along the foreshore with views towards Grange, Holme Island and Hampsfell before passing Arnside Coastguard station -- of which I am an auxiliary member. Continuing towards Newbarns farmyard, they go through woodland and a caravan park to arrive at White Creek and onto the sands. This walk is more

(Opposite) *Children of all ages understandably love the cross-Bay walk, running ahead of the adults or splashing in the water. In the bottom picture, Cedric is perhaps wondering if he will have to rescue a very young participant! (Paul Nickson; John Briggs)*

(This page) *The railway provides a much more direct route across the Kent estuary than the road, and thus is regularly used by walkers. In this August 2002 scene, Kents Bank station is almost swamped by a huge crowd who have completed the crossing and are about to return to Arnside by train. The chances of them all getting a seat seem remote. It used to be possible for extra coaches to be requested, but unhappily those days are gone. (John Briggs)*

suitable for all age groups and that is why it has become so popular.

There is very little difference in mileage, although on the map it is only about four miles as the crow flies. We cannot fly so we go where it is safe - and that means a lot of meandering which adds to the mileage. A tractor and a covered trailer with seating accommodation is always on hand out in the Bay for those who at any stage of the walk decide they cannot complete the journey to the shore. I find that the passengers on the trailer are usually young children - not because they are tired but because this is a novelty ride across Morecambe Bay. Enjoyment to the full!

Questions I am often asked

Very seldom does anyone ask questions at the start of a walk. People come up to me once we arrive on the sands, and always when we have stops out there to gather together.

1. Can we ask you some questions, please?
2. Where are the quicksands?
3. Has anyone ever died out there?
4. Do you ever get frightened?
5. How do you know where to go and how did you learn this knowledge?
6. Have you ever been stuck in quicksands?
7. How deep is the river crossing?
8. How long have you been doing the walks?
9. Have you ever met the Queen?
10. Has Her Majesty ever been across the sands?
11. What time is low water?
12. At what time will the tide be here today?
13. Do you ever get fed up with leading the walks?
14. What will happen when you decide to call it a day?

I answer all of these sensible and interesting questions in turn. Walkers seem to appreciate this, and I enjoy it too, as it appears to put them at ease.

Crossings in the Past

Centuries before the Morecambe Bay Walk as such was established, travellers were crossing the sands in order to shorten the distance to Furness. If all was well, the sand would be firm and the river fordable but a petition to the King from the Abbot of Furness in 1326 suggests that this was not often the case. He asked for a coroner to investigate the great loss of life on the sands.

The first record of a Guide is in 1501 when one Edmonstone was described as 'Carter upon Kent Sands'. The Prior of Cartmel paid his successor, William Gate, although responsibility for payment later passed to Conishead Priory, near Ulverston. The future looked bleak, however, when the Abbot of Furness was charged with treason for involvement in the Pilgrimage of Grace in 1536. The dissolution of the monasteries followed almost at once and the vast Furness Abbey, the largest Cisterian foundation in the county, was surrendered with all its wealth. In 1540 its entire estates were transferred to the Duchy of Lancaster, which took on many of its obligations including payment for the Guide at Guide's Farm.

The earliest Duchy Patent dates from 1548 and granted Thomas Hodgson the office of Guide 'with one tenement in Kents-Bank in Cartmel, which was called Carte Hows, with three closes of land to the same adjacent'. For the next three hundred years succeeding generations of the Carter family came to hold the post and there is even a suggestion that the Hodgsons may have adapted the surname 'Carter' to cement their occupation identity.

It does seem weird to write about the previous Guides in terms of office - all of whom lived at Guide's Farm and sat in the same room where this book has been written. What did they think about being a Guide? Did they realise how important it was? They would not have believed so many people could have crossed the Bay in the last forty years.

Why so many of the earlier Guides were described as 'Carters of the Sands' is difficult to determine. Their duty was to be in attendance at the fords, which they were bound to discover on the ebb tide, and conduct persons across safely. It appears that the Guides used to have a horse and cart at the edge of the rivers to covey foot passengers. This must have been more comfortable than wading through water with a strong current, especially in the winter months when the rivers would be icy cold. Horsemen were seldom able to cross without taking their feet out of the stirrups and raising them to escape a wetting. Those who were particular about the condition of their stirrups lifted them out of their saddles to prevent the salt water ruining them!

Many famous people have crossed the Bay. In 1759 the evangelist John Wesley made the journey, as did George Fox, the celebrated founder of the Quakers - the Society of Friends. Thomas Gray (1716 - 1771), one of the greatest English poets and the writer of the famous 'Elegy in a Country Churchyard', crossed the sands twice, once in 1767 and again in 1769 on tours of the Lake District.

On his 1769 visit, Gray walked down from Lancaster where he was staying to what was then the pretty village of Poulton (now Morecambe). An old man mending his fishing nets told him of the dangers of crossing the sands, and also a very moving story of how a cockle fisherman was driving a little cart with his two grown-up daughters accompanied by his wife on horseback. They set out to cross the sands as they had done frequently in the past, but when they were about half way over a thick fog came down and the water became much deeper than expected.

The old man was puzzled; he stopped and said he would go on a little way to find some mark or

(Opposite) Cross-Bay carriage drives evoke the days when a horse-and-cart was the normal way of travelling over the sands. In the upper picture, members of the Ribble Valley Driving Club are coming ashore at Kents Bank, while in the lower photograph there is much activity in the spray near Arnside. (Fred Broomfield; Terry Carter)

(This page) The building of Kent viaduct, prominent in this view of a group of walkers setting off from Arnside, radically changed the nature of the estuary. Opening of the railway in 1857 also massively reduced the amount of traffic across the Bay, although it did not prevent a tragedy in the same year when at least ten young men were drowned. (Gary Taylor)

Guides from 1501

Edmondstone	1501	(1)
William Gate	1535	(2)
Thomas Hodgson	1548	
Richard Carter	? - 1564	(3)
William Carter	1564 - 1592	
William Carter	1592 - 1602	
Edward Carter	1602 - 1633	
Edward Carter	1633 - 1644	
William Carter	1644 - 1649	
Thomas Carter	1649 - 1661	(4)
William Carter	1661 - 1672	(5)
J. Carter	?	
John Carter	c1680 - 1718	
John Carter	1718 - 1746	
John Carter	1746 - 1780	
William Carter	1780 - 1799	
William Carter	1800 - 1828	
James Carter	1828 - 1856	
John Carter	1856 - 1867	
John Nevison	1867 - 1875	(6)
George Sedgwick	1875 - 1919	
Jack Burrow	1919 - 1943	
Jack Burrow	1943 - 1950	(7)
William Burrow	1950 - 1963	
Cedric Robinson	1963 -	

1. 'Carter upon Kent Sands'
2. Paid by the Prior of Cartmel
3. Name possibly taken from the place where he lived - 'Carter House'
4. In 1660 guided the people taking George Fox to prison
5. Drowned in the course of his duty
6. Dismissed
7. Son of former guide

- brought them back to the land alive but they were so frightened with terror and distress that for many days they were unable to give an account of themselves. The bodies of their parents were found on the next ebb tide, that of the father being only a few paces distant from the spot where he had left them.

A tragedy occurred in 1857 when at least ten and probably twelve young men were lost in an accident on the sands. The majority of them were returning home on completion of their service as farm labourers, and no doubt in happy and boisterous spirits at the prospect of seeing their friends and enjoying a holiday. It had been the custom for young men from this district, engaged in work over the sands, to meet together at Whitsuntide in order to accompany each other home again. There appears to have been such an arrangement on this occasion because William Benson of Flookburgh had agreed with George Ashburner, carter, that a horse and cart would be available to bring these young men across.

Fishermen at Silverdale who were out on the night in question heard the men's voices as they proceeded on their way. Yet about a mile off shore, full of life and anticipating a brief relaxation from toil, they were all pitched out of the cart and drowned. At the inquest it emerged that the party had paused in the tap room of the Royal Oak public house at Allithwaite before setting off across the sands. Questioned whether the driver of the cart was drunk, a witness replied, 'He was not correct in that way. He was not drunk but what they call sharp fresh.'

An enquiry was held at Grange in April 1873 as to the suitability of John Nevison, the then Guide, and whether it was worth continuing the appointment in view of the declining cross-sands traffic. At the hearing, which found in favour of retention, it was alleged that Nevison 'often spent whole days drinking at Dickinson's public house at Allithwaite'. The lengthy report of the proceedings in the Lancashire Guardian contains so much of interest that I have included it as an Appendix.

other with which he was familiar. The others stayed a while waiting for him to return. They called aloud but no reply came. At last the young women pressed their mother to think where they were and go on. She would not move from the place nor would she leave her horse and get into the cart with them. After much time was wasted they decided to turn back and gave themselves up to the guidance of the horses.

The elder woman was soon washed off and perished but the girls clung close to their cart. Its horse - sometimes wading and sometimes swimming

Famous Occasions

Had the decision of the 1873 enquiry gone the other way, it is interesting to reflect that I would not have been able to write this book. Nor would I have had the pleasure of guiding many famous people across the sands. The most memorable occasion occurred in 1985.

The Duke of Edinburgh

May 30th 1985 was for me a very special crossing as I accompanied the Duke of Edinburgh in the royal carriage, along with ten other horse-drawn carriages following close behind on the only route possible at that time. This was from Silverdale to Kents Bank, with the Duke driving a magnificent team of four horses to a sturdy Marathon vehicle.

I had guided thousands of people across Morecambe Bay but this was something totally different from any crossing before. A great deal of preparation went into this event so that everything would run as smoothly as possible. The sands and the River Kent were unstable with constant movement but eventually they did settle down to make the crossing feasible. There were press interviews at Holker Hall, the home of Lord and Lady Cavendish and family, and at Kents Bank Hotel and Guide's Farm as well as several meetings with the Lancashire and Cumbria police forces. The organisers had to keep the whole occasion under wraps until it was officially announced from Buckingham Palace that the Duke would be taking part and it was really going to happen, as this was one man's decision.

After going out onto the sands very early at 3.30am to make a final check before the crossing in the afternoon, I was very pleased with what I found and turned for home as the sun rose, knowing that we were in for a perfect day. I had now made my decision for the drive to go ahead and it was all systems go! It was a truly memorable event, not just for Olive, myself and our family and friends, but for all the thousands of people who turned out on the day to watch this historic occasion.

Lord Bragg

It started with a phone call from Melvyn Bragg's London office asking if it would be possible for me to accompany him on a walk across the Bay. A date was chosen and we were to meet up at Morecambe Lodge Farm at Bolton-le-Sands, very near to Hest Bank railway station.

My daughter Jean drove me round to the other side of the Bay and as we arrived we noticed a parked vehicle. A figure stepped out and came towards me as I was preparing myself for the walk, changing into trainers as the sand looked hard and dry at the start. I did not recognise Melvyn at first as he was wearing casual clothes - trainers and a pair of jeans and looked nothing like he appeared when seen on television. A few words were exchanged - yes, this was Melvyn and now we were both ready for the crossing.

It was a glorious day for the walk over to Kents Bank. As the high sun hit the sand, you could scarcely bear to look. It was like a sheet of silver spread out across the open Bay. The gulls, oystercatchers and the singing cockles were all to be seen and heard on this most beautiful mid-May afternoon by just the two of us. The Lakeland fells were clearly visible and at their best and we would see lots more as this was to be a four-hour journey. With the breeze coming from the south-west the clouds soon cleared and left us with lovely blue skies so that which ever way we looked it was as pretty as a picture.

(This page) Television and film companies come to Morecambe Bay in ever-increasing numbers to record celebrities completing the walk or to make educational productions and documentaries. Here members of a film unit are clinging gamely to Cedric's tractor as they come ashore at Kents Bank. (Fred Broomfield)

(Opposite) It is scarcely surprising that the Bay is so popular with film companies. Whether in daytime with distant clouds (top), or during one of its spectacular sunsets (lower), it is matched by few places in the world for its ever-changing sands and skies. (Cedric Robinson)

Melvyn asked me questions continually and my main topic was fishing and the pleasure of it, but we also discussed the Bay and the sands themselves. I was able to explain where new channels were about to be formed, where 'bracks' (breakaways of sand in the rivers and dykes) were suspect where quicksands threatened and the sad stories of loss of life. The reason Melvyn wished to accompany me on a walk was to get the sensation of being on the Bay, which he wanted to convey in a book he was about to write entitled *The Maid of Buttermere*. He could not have come on a more ideal day and I did enjoy his company.

Although my estimate of the crossing time was four hours, it did in fact take us five and a half with the continual stopping to ask questions and look around. The River Kent was awesome, very wide and almost thigh deep. Melvyn is not quite as tall as I am but we both got a wetting, although we soon dried out in the warm sun and the breeze. At the finish as we came up towards the railway station, Melvyn thanked me and said how much he had enjoyed the experience, but he was certainly tired and his legs were beginning to ache. He told me that when he was up in the Lakes he walked the fells and regarded himself as fit, but walking the sands was something he would never forget.

Melvyn later wrote an article in *Punch* about his experience of crossing the sands, from which the following extract is taken:

"There are people you meet who come straight out of a book, even in our sophisticated times when such a nice and simple phrase might seem rarer than a Nigerian Turnip, even in our television age (when actually more books are read, but let that pass) when we are collectively accused of reneging on the fine print. Even so, these people exist, only sometimes as 'characters' and they can step out of the pages and into your life without so much as a (book) token of acknowledgement, of the difference between life and fiction.

I met a man the other day. He led me across the sands of Morecambe Bay. Cedric Robinson is the Queen's Guide to the sands, but also takes the title of Sand Pilot. It is a title which evokes the ancient and the romantic. Pilot has been an inspiration, a metaphor, a hope.

Tennyson - 'I hope to see my Pilot face to face when I have crossed the bar' and those who bear that title inherit an ancient Kingdom of Trust. You feel some of that as you trudge out across the Morecambe Bay Sands.

When Wordsworth resettled in the Lakes on Christmas Eve, 1799, it was a place in which those binding nourishing rural communities and those open plain but heroic people who are the most cherished characters, and in his work could still be found. For Wordsworth they had links with Arcadia, and with the deep decency of an honest endeavour which encountered the largest claims with stoicism and drear sustenance, even Solace from nature. 'Michael' is the most vivid of these creations - a shepherd whose only son abandoned him for the corrupting city and left him without an heir, without hope, stricken down but always a man of worth.

I suspect that Cedric Robinson would find such an introduction and such a comparison embarrassing, but it is there. If you know the Lakes and knew Wordsworth then you have met him before and he does not let you down.

Even his turn of phrase reaches back 'And it was done......And so we did' - while his appearance, strong, thatched grey hair, cheeks apple ripe with the weather, movement at once steady and alert - comes straight from resolution and independence."

Bill Bryson

When you meet Bill Bryson you soon feel that you have known him all your life. He is so friendly and approachable and laid back, but he is also very witty. The plan was for Bill and his TV crew to join me on the shore at Kents Bank for a walk with a small group of excited locals. It was a nice clear day but there was a very cold wind. Bill told me that he never felt entirely comfortable with British seaside weather, even on the sunniest of days in summer, so I arranged for my nephew Kenny to have my tractor and Sandpiper trailer at the ready to give them more confidence.

Bill said that he grew up almost a thousand miles from the nearest sea and the reason why he liked Morecambe Bay so much was that it was compact and pretty. Much of the time there was not much water in it at all - and that was his kind of bay! One other thing he found hard to understand was why so many people just sat on the edge of the Bay. It was certain to be chilly and damp and a long way from toilets, and there was nothing to do but huddle behind a windbreak and gaze out into a cold grey sea.

Bill had a conversation with one of the group, a nice man who had retired into Grange from Rochdale. He was wearing a pair of low-cut shoes with socks and carrying a thumb-stick. He enjoyed talking to Bill and, as he had been on the sands with me before, he described the sands and the river crossing so well that you would have thought that he had known them all his life.

'There is always one!' commented Bill. 'They are there to tell you that what you are about to do is not as you imagined. The River Kent could in fact be at least three hundred yards across and come well up to your knees if you are lucky - and can be much deeper - and so amazingly these people always carry a stick. On the other hand, and he would be corrected if he were wrong, he had been looking forward to this walk so much today - until he was given my book Sand Pilot of Morecambe Bay. Some words in the book put doubt in his mind as he read, "Across the sands of Morecambe Bay the tide advances faster than a man can run, quicksands and ever-changing channels have in the past claimed countless lives. And now it is not uncommon for holidaymakers to find themselves in difficulty."'

The doubt in his mind changed when I spoke to the group and this seemed to give him more confidence. It was to be quite a while before we met up with the River Kent. As we walked we chatted, stopped occasionally and filmed, and he thought it odd to reflect that a few hours earlier the spot where we were now walking had been under at least twenty feet of water. The one disappointment was that we could not walk straight across the Bay to Morecambe because of deep water! Too deep to wade and too wide to swim, so now instead we had to turn left towards Arnside and the Kent. Here at last was what everyone had been waiting for - the river crossing.

From here it looks positively enormous and very, very wide. I jokingly shouted ahead to the group, 'Any non-swimmers?' The tractor was alongside us just in case. Bill had very few rules in life, so he said, but one of them was - never wade across a body of water when you could not see to the other side. Another was - never immerse yourself in anything colder than liquid nitrogen.

As we walked into the river I could not stop myself from laughing as I saw the look on most of the group's faces. Bill said he could feel his bones cracking and the odd pained numbness with the sensation that his toes were about to fall off. Someone in the group spoke and Bill said, 'He didn't really say that this was lovely, did he?' When we arrived safely at the other side, Bill took the shoulder of someone so as not to lose his balance, emptied out the water from his wellies and then put them back on again!

We now took a line for White Creek, which was the last leg of the sand journey. This took us about twenty minutes. As we walked up towards Newbarn's Caravan Park and on to much higher ground, we looked back over the way we had come and it was so clear that the views were really outstanding. Crossing the Kent was now the topic of conversation and everyone of us had a good laugh when Bill told us that the producer was probably sitting quite comfortably in a warm pub somewhere in Arnside waiting for us!

(This page) Cedric has had the pleasure of meeting many celebrities and often guiding them across the sands. Here he is with Alan Titchmarsh in May 2003. (Roger Arnold)

(Opposite) Cedric with staff and whistle at the ready, as so often portrayed on television and film. This photgraph was taken off Arnside Point in August 2002. (John Briggs)

Film & TV

There was now wide interest by television companies interested in filming out there in Morecambe Bay. It is the perfect location and most of the time - weather permitting - is surely a photographer's dream. There are few places in the world to equal the Bay with its beautiful sunrises and sunsets, ever-changing sands and fascinating tides. There are also quicksands...

The 'body' on the sands

Professor Magnus Pike was on television with a programme called 'Don't Ask Me'. Members of the audience could put questions about almost anything and some bright spark asked him, 'What makes quicksands?' No expense was spared and the programme was filmed by Yorkshire Television. This is going back some years, and the young and very enthusiastic producer at that time was Barry Cockcroft, whom my wife Olive and I came to know quite well over the years.

At first a researcher, a young lass of no more than about twenty years of age, came along to Guide's Farm to find out just what these quicksands were all about. I took her over Cart Lane railway crossing and down onto the foreshore after she had donned a pair of Olive's green wellies. I explained as much as I could and then asked if she was game for it. She replied, 'That's why I am here Mr Robinson.' So I took her by the hand, said 'don't stop whatever', and, as the surface of the sand bent and buckled, and showed signs of cracking open, we raced across and onto firm terrain. She said afterwards how really frightened she had been but thought that this would make a very good film. And it did.

A lot went into the making of the film, including a rescue attempt by a very large orange-coloured air-sea rescue helicopter. It was difficult lifting the man from the sands even with all that power and at one stage the procedure did not go according to plan. The suction was so great that the rope slung around the victim's arms was pulling the helicopter down, which was really frightening to watch. Then all of a sudden, release, and up he came slowly - and the helicopter made its way across the Bay and back towards Yorkshire with a man dangling on the end of a rope!

That is not the end of the story - Oh no! After the experts back at Yorkshire Television studios had studied the film, they decided that the man had not gone down far enough into the quicksands and thus it did not look sufficiently dangerous. So they rang me and told me this! They could not get anyone else to take part in the film by walking over the quicksands as word had got around as to how hazardous they were! I suggested to them that they should make a dummy and, as long as it was heavy enough, it should sink quite easily.

The second visit with the dummy went perfectly. The lower half from the waist was made of steel and the upper parts of wood and it looked almost real. It had to be held so that it did not topple, so I volunteered and laid down flat over the quicksands just out of camera shot. Down he went, up to the waist, as the camera rolled and everyone watching was so pleased. The shoots from this scene were put together with the earlier ones, edited, and were a great success.

The only thing now was that the camera crew were all safely back in Yorkshire and there was a 'man' stuck in the quicksands! Almost every household in Kents Bank and Grange has clear views of the Bay, so our telephone was now ringing non-stop with callers very worried about what they could see out there as the tide was coming in.

I said to Olive, 'This has got to stop!' So as the tide ebbed, I took my old bushman saw out of the shed, and after giving Olive a kiss and her telling me to be very careful, I went down the lane, over the railway crossing and onto the sands. The man was still there - he had not moved a jot. I got wet through laying flat down on to the sands, gritted my teeth and started sawing him off by his waist.

Coming back safely up the shore, I felt really good about what I had just done. At least now the phone would stop ringing about the 'man' in the quicksands, but just imagine someone walking their dog along the shoreline one day and suddenly coming across part of a body washed up by the tide. It could have proved very frightening - but I never heard of anything being found.

'Cut, Mr Robinson!'
In October 1974 I had quite a part to play in a film called 'Lakeland Summer' which was shown on BBC TV's 'Pebble Mill at One'. My role was to re-enact a Guide in the past and to forsake my old tractor for one of my favourite ponies - a palomino gelding. The idea was to be filmed on horseback marking out the route and guiding a team of horses pulling a very old-fashioned carriage across the sands to Grange.

Cheyenne, my pony, was quite a handful when he was unloaded from the horsebox on the foreshore at Morecambe Lodge Farm, near Hest Bank. He was like a two-year old and would not stand still while being saddled up. On our way over the sands to the place we were to start the filming he bucked all the way!

I was to mark the route with laurel bushes, but whenever I dismounted and worked one into the sand Cheyenne walked forward, got hold with his teeth and out came the bush! He showed me up continually. The direction from the producer was now quite frequent, 'Cut, Mr Robinson, can we have that scene again please.' Yes, I have some treasured memories of being filmed out on the Bay. Bob Langley was the interviewer and he rode across in style in that lovely old carriage.

It was nice to hear again from BBC TV in February 1975 with news that 'Lakeland Summer' had been a huge success. A repeat programme was to be shown and would go out as three twenty-five minute films in April. I thought this was great, but never in a million years did I ever want to be a budding actor and stand in front of a television camera with lots of unrehearsed questions to be answered. However, I was now beginning to enjoy the set-up and provided it was about the sands or something connected with them, I was quite happy to go along with whatever they suggested.

'Sand Pilot'
My first book *Sand Pilot of Morecambe Bay* was published in 1980 and Olive and me, my whole family, neighbours and friends were thrilled to bits over it. A respectable person from Grange had told me in conversation that this just did not happen unless you were well known. Me, being green as grass, thought that anyone could get a script published, without any problems. Anyway, maybe I was lucky and I proved them wrong, but the publishers were well pleased and gave it plenty of publicity nationally.

Lots of signing sessions were organised for me to attend and the first was at the station bookstall in Grange. I was sat there enjoying myself and things were going really well when a call came through from Granada Television at Manchester. They wanted me to travel to their studios and would provide a taxi there and back. Times of arrival were given to me and I was told my interviewer would be Bob Smithies. I could not wait to tell Olive about this and she and all the family were only too pleased for me to go.

I had not previously met Bob Smithies and did not know what to expect. The temperature inside so hot that I could feel my face getting redder and redder by the minute. Bob did not waste much time after the handshake and led me to the powder room. When he opened the door I could not help but notice well-known names such as Elsie Tanner written above the dressing table

(This page) *When Cedric's first book* Sand Pilot of Morecambe Bay *was published in 1980, the whole family, neighbours and friends were 'thrilled to bits over it'. A special celebration included a suitably iced cake.*

(Opposite, top) *Cedric and Olive, photographed during the event.*

(Lower) *When the book was re-published in 1998, a new foreword was written by Hannah Hauxwell, who accompanied Cedric to all the signing sessions. She is on the right in this group photograph taken at Guide's Farm. (Fred Broomfield -3)*

mirrors. 'Take a seat,' said Bob, 'anywhere will do' - so I sat in front of one of those large mirrors. Bob did the same, but I think he had his own special chair.

The next thing I knew we were both being made up to appear before the television cameras. I needed much more make-up than Bob because by this time you could have boiled a kettle on my head! I was powdered, eyebrows trimmed and sticking-out bits lopped from my hair. I emerged looking like and feeling like a circus clown!

All seemed to go to plan and I came home to a wonderful surprise party that Olive and family had organised for me. They had invited our good friends and neighbours so there was quite a house full. She had made a special cake in the shape of an open book with the title across the top icing. We all had more than a happy hour, a really great time with such a lovely buffet. It was a memorable send off for the new book.

The second meeting with Bob was an invitation for us both to attend a dinner given by Granada Television at the Tythe Barn Restaurant at Garstang where we met many TV celebrities. Bob has now retired from television but a few years ago he rang and asked if it would be possible for me to accompany him, his wife and a few friends on a walk across the Bay from Arnside to Kents Bank which of course I agreed to do. The walk was at a relaxing pace and, with being just a few of us, we were able to walk and talk and even stop from time to time to take photographs. The day was just perfect for us and we could not have enjoyed ourselves more.

When *Sand Pilot of Morecambe Bay* was re-published in 1998, Hannah Hauxwell wrote a new foreword. She had become a good friend as a result of earlier visits to Kents Bank when on holiday, but now she stayed with us for a week and accompanied Olive and me to all the signing sessions, which she enjoyed. We also travelled to Radio Blackburn and the two of us broadcast live on the same subject. At the time there was a heavy snowfall and I was hoping and praying that it would not last. Luckily it disappeared almost as fast as it came down and we were able to travel home in safety.

Sir Harry Secombe

By the early 1980s there was more interest than ever in making short films centred on the Bay. Border Television arranged for me to be filmed with Sir Harry Secombe for the programme 'Highway - Morecambe Bay'. He was one of the nicest persons one could ever wish to meet. In August 1989 I had to provide filming facilities for the cross-Bay walk from Arnside to Kents Bank, and if it turned out to be wet we would film early in September. Later in September I was to have my tractor and trailer at Kents Bank station to take part in various sequences to be included in the programme.

Harry rang me from Kents Bank on the day we were about to be filmed saying that he had done his stint - and now it was my turn so could I get down to the station as soon as possible! When I arrived he was standing at the door of a vehicle about the size of a caravan. He beckoned me over and said, 'Come inside, Cedric, sit yourself down.' There were several people in the van who were all introduced to me. Harry asked, 'How's the old eye doing Cedric?' - he knew I had had an operation for a detached retina. When I replied that it seemed to be doing nicely, he surprised me by saying, 'Oh but don't be too sure about that Cedric. I have a good pal who had the same operation and he has been falling over himself ever since.' When I asked who it was, he smiled and then replied, 'Spike Milligan.' I took him to be serious but he was just pulling my leg!

We travelled out onto the sands in Sandpiper, my tractor-drawn covered trailer driven by my good friend Larry. Despite the very windy weather on that day, filming went well and it was such a pleasure to be out on the sands in the company of Sir Harry Secombe.

More personalities

There have been many other visits by film crews down the years. Two very well known TV personalities, Victoria Wood and 'Hayley' from Coronation Street, crossed the sands under my guidance. Victoria was accompanied by a minder and wore a peaked hat well down over her eyes so that she would not be recognised. Haley was not so cautious and made friends with everyone. After the walk was over she obliged many people by signing her autograph or even having a photograph taken with them. This was a sponsored walk to raise money to help fight Parkinson's disease as Hayley's father was a sufferer.

Alistair Macdonald, regularly on TV at one time with Stuart Hall, was the first interviewer to come all the way across the Bay together with a camera crew who filmed the walk. It was a perfect day for it. We started out from Hest Bank and finished on the promenade at Grange.

The long-running holiday programme 'Wish you were here' with Judith Chalmers was filmed from Kents Bank and out in the Bay. Judith and her entourage travelled round to this side of the Bay from Morecambe after being filmed on the funfair. Out we went onto the sands with my tractor and trailer until we came to the River Kent, where the crew lost no time in setting up their gear. There was a cameraman, the soundman, two or three other blokes who just seemed to walk back and forth to the tractor and trailer, and the continuity person. You learn a lot from these people when you are out with them quite frequently. The filming went extraordinarily well, with Judith being well pleased with herself after chasing me up and down in the river, or was it the other way round? It is so long ago since the filming took place that I am not quite so sure!

Another of my visits out onto the sands to be filmed was in October 1987 in the interesting company of David Bellamy. It was for a Yorkshire Television children's programme called 'Bellamy's Bugle'.

'Blue Peter' was one of the first programmes to be filmed in the Bay with Simon Groom driving my tractor. Goldie, their dog, loved being out on the sands as it was quite a change for him not to be filmed in the studio.

'Treasure Hunt' was filmed in Morecambe Bay from a helicopter. I was driven out to the location on a horse-drawn carriage, the area chosen being about four miles out from Kents Bank. Anneka Rice was not available for this series so Anabelle Croft took her place. George Bowman from Penrith came down with his team of horses, which took part in the filming. The helicopter did eventually find us out in the Bay and I had previously marked out a circle with laurels where it was safe for it to land. I had to hide the clue in the sand, marked with a laurel twig. Anabelle had to enlist my help in finding the clue, once down on the sands, but as the studio contestants guided her around the course it was difficult for me to know her exact time of arrival. Eventually I was spotted and filming went ahead as planned

On another occasion I was again being filmed for television and this time the interviewer was Paul Heiney. Morecambe Bay was shown from a different angle, as I was filmed leaving Grange by Crown Hill and taking the footpath known as Bailey Lane. This leads you very steeply down to the railway crossing and promenade and out onto the sands. The only thing was that the cameraman had to be a few paces in front of me and walking backwards, which must have been very difficult for him. I kept thinking to myself, 'Any minute now and he'll fall over himself.' But he didn't, and we carried on to do the interview out in the Bay.

In April 1995 I was asked if I would take part in a documentary film about the Marijushri Mahayana Buddhist Centre at Conishead Priory, near Ulverston. It was a very early hour in the morning when filming took place out in the Bay near Chapel Island and it was very cold. I was with two Buddhists who were wearing only their thin wraps and must have been starved to death.

(This page) After filming by American TV in July 1997, the group adjourned to the Guide over Sands public house at Allithwaite. Cedric had the honour of pulling the first pint when the pub - formerly known as The Royal Oak - was renovated and renamed. On the left of this picture with his wife Christine is Larry Bennett, who once famously rescued Cedric and six hundredweight of cockles from a broken-down van on the M6 in the middle of the night.

(Opposite) Judith Chalmers with Cedric's grandson Simon, photographed on Morecambe Bay during the filming of her long-running holiday programme 'Wish you were here'. After all this time Cedric insists that he cannot remember whether she chased him up and down the River Kent or if it was the other way round! (Fred Broomfield -2)

As we came ashore we were interviewed at great length, and I was glad to get back into the car and warm myself up. After a few months I was sent a finished videotape, which they called 'The Guide', together with a letter of thanks. All of us at Guide's Farm found the video most interesting.

I had often watched Fred, the TV Weatherman, jump across the water and land on the floating map of the British Isles, sometimes almost falling in! He came to Grange in February 1997 and drove his favourite little red bubble car along the promenade where we met and were filmed together. In May the same year I was recorded on video for the archives of the British History Trust.

I was again filmed in July by American TV to show the dangers of quicksands out in the Bay.

Their interviewer was Eric Strauss who had a really strong American accent. When filming was over it was suggested that we all went out for a meal to the 'Guide over Sands' public house at Allithwaite. I had previously been invited by the brewery to pull the first pint at this newly renovated pub, which used to be called 'The Royal Oak'. That evening we all had a first-class meal.

The list of people from different television and radio companies who have been out on the sands and put together short films, educational productions and documentaries over the years seems endless. Yet I must say that most of the time I enjoyed meeting with these enthusiasts and being able to take part.

Crossings with a difference

Many of my most memorable crossings have not involved celebrities but nevertheless have been equally interesting and rewarding.

The Battle of White Creek

A walk that I led across the Bay in June 1974 stands out in my mind as being the most colourful I have ever recorded. I received a letter from the Roundheads' Association asking me to lead an army of Cavaliers across the sands to White Creek, Arnside. Here they were to meet up at and to do battle with the Roundheads in the first re-enactment of its kind.

The Cavaliers assembled over on the shore at Cart Lane crossing before moving out in style across the Bay. The day was beautiful and so were the women's costumes - pretty bonnets, blouses of various colours and style, with long white cotton skirts and leather footwear. The men, being soldiers, were in full battle uniform with their lances held upright and were wearing long boots made in leather. I thought it was a pity to cross the sands, and especially the River Kent, as their beautiful costumes would never be the same again once they had gone through the water.

A good friend of mine, Mrs Hirst, asked if she could come along on this special day and watch the battle. Our daughter Jean and her friend Deirdre went with her for company.

The crossing went wonderfully well, in a military kind of style, on the approach to White Creek. Hidden from view were the Roundheads and their sign for battle to commence was some very loud cannon fire. Mrs Hirst, Jean, Deirdre and I all ran for cover and watched from a distance - a very safe one as now all hell was let loose with such a noise. People were screaming and shouting and it was a pitched battle that went on for some time.

From where we stood, this battle certainly looked for real and some of them did get hurt. We never did find out who won because it became time for me and my three onlookers to make our way back across the river before the tide turned. Coming ashore at Cart Lane, Mrs Hirst was so thrilled at being able to cross the sands and record this colourful event on camera that she gave me a set of photographs that I still treasure.

Under sail

In September 1974 I received a letter asking me to accompany a man and his Chinese Wheelbarrow or Desert Cart from one side of the Bay to the other - a distance of about nine or ten miles, depending on which way the wind is blowing. It was a lightweight affair with a wheel five feet in diameter and a long narrow box on either side to carry the load.

The distribution of the load in this way put the weight on the cart and not on the driver. A sail was used to take advantage of any favourable wind, leaving only the guiding of the cart to the driver and enabling him to cover many more miles than would have been the case had he had to push or pull the load of a conventional cart.

The whole idea was to test the cart in the stringent conditions of the Bay before taking it out to the Sahara Desert for a further test, after which it was hoped to put it into production. It was seen as a potential benefit to desert people, who could not afford to use motorised transport or camels to move their wares. The vehicle was to be manufactured by a well-known British firm and a BBC 'Nationwide' helicopter covered the Morecambe Bay test.

Although the trials seemed to go well in the Bay, it was apparently a different matter when the cart reached the Sahara where the fluctuations in wind strength are much greater. The cart had to be held firmly against the wind, but if this suddenly dropped it would then be over on its side. The wheels were found to be too narrow and, all in all, the going was extremely hard. The journey of two thousand miles took three months. Eventually it was decided not to put the cart into production, but the prototype is preserved in store at the Science Museum, South Kensington.

A gaggle of geese

I suppose one of the most unusual requests came in July 2000 from Lucy Muller, a young woman farmer from Whitby. She wanted to raise money for a twelve-year old arthritis sufferer by walking with seventeen geese, starting on the west coast at Furness Abbey and crossing the Bay before continuing right across the country to finish at Whitby. She achieved her goal and I think the highlight of her journey must have been the Morecambe Bay section.

I took my two youngest granddaughters, Amy and Danielle, along with me as we set off at quite a pace with the geese close behind, making our way out into the open space of the Bay and on towards the River Kent crossing. Everything went well and we all came towards the end of this unusual crossing of the sands by finishing at White Creek, Arnside. I believe this was the next stopping place for the night. My job over for the day, we turned back the way we had come out and made our way back home.

(Opposite, top) One of the most unusual crossings was in July 2000, when farmer Lucy Muller raised money for an arthritis sufferer by driving seventeen geese across England from Furness Abbey to Whitby via Morecambe Bay. Here they are waddling off in great style, with Cedric accompanied by Danielle Nickson (left) and Amy Robinson (right)

(Lower) The gaggle soon assumed an orderly formation once out in the Bay! The horse was to provide water and corn for the geese. (Paul Nickson - 2)

'Keeper of the Kingdom'

In August 1997 Olive received a phone call from a Julian Calder, a London photographer who had just come from Buckingham Palace after speaking with the Queen and Prince Philip. If it was convenient for us, he would travel up to Grange-over-Sands by rail that very same day and hopefully get some good shots out in the Bay for a book by Alastair Bruce of Crionaich entitled Keepers of the Kingdom

The weather was perfect and the evening light even better still. Julian Calder and I set out from Guide's Farm on my tractor at five-thirty in the evening and did not arrive back at the farm until nine. He then had to travel back to London by train. The picture chosen for the book was hung in the National Portrait Gallery in London for an exhibition. Olive and I received invitations to go to the preview but unfortunately we were unable to attend owing to other commitments.

Every month of the year

Jim Lowther from Preston came to be a regular figure out on the sands at weekends and we came to know each other so well as he hardly missed coming on a walk. Jim was a loner and would rather cross the sands on his own. Then he met up and made friends with Gordon Handslip, a retired grocer from Grange who was born in 1893 and made his first crossing on in August 1955.

Gordon is the only person to have accompanied Jim Lowther across Morecambe Bay in every month of the year, but Jim told me that he had him worried at times. Gordon was nevertheless a remarkable man and when he was eighty-four he walked from Hest Bank to Grange in 3 hours 10 minutes. His last crossing with Jim was in September 1980 when he was aged eighty-seven but he lived for another ten years until April 1990/

Sadly I have just heard that Jim, a friend for forty years, has died at the age of seventy-three. I had not seen him out in the Bay quite so frequently during the last two or three years and did hear that he had not been too well. The Bay is not the kind of place you expect to meet up with someone unless you are on a guided walk or perhaps come across a lone fisherman from Flookburgh on his old tractor. I always looked forward to seeing Jim and having a chat, usually about the meandering River Kent that he had crossed so many times. He was so knowledgeable. On lots of occasions I would see him treading in the river catching flukes, the tasty flatfish he would take home for his tea. Jim was a very private person, who will be sadly missed by all who had the pleasure of being in his company.

Trousers down!

As my cross-Bay walks were about to start in April 2003, I received a phone call from Harry Brown at Torrisholme, near Morecambe. Olive knew him from years ago when his family lived in Ravenstown. Harry told me of a relative who was keen to do the walk but was very nervous of water, and had been so all her life. I told Harry to pass a message on to her saying that if she came along to make herself known to me, I would escort her personally through the river arm in arm. In fact, I would look after her.

She came and just before crossing the Kent, as there was quite a strong breeze and the river was about knee high, I asked her if she would mind holding my stick and haversack while I rolled up my trousers. Everyone was now ready for the off and as I blew my whistle I put my arm around hers to make her feel secure. I kept asking her if she was all right and she replied 'so far', -and then when I looked at her she did look rather frightened. The river was a long way from one side to the other - about three hundred yards.

I said, 'Don't look down at the river whatever, just set your eyes on the far bank and you will be all right.' We came out of the river and I said to the lady, 'Would you mind holding my stick and my bag while I pull my trousers down?' She was quick in replying, 'I might have known you would want something in return!'
I could not help laughing at what she had said

and after the walk Harry rang us to tell us of how much his relative had enjoyed herself. Who knows? - She may want to come again next year.

Morecambe Bay by night

One unforgettable experience is still talked about to this day. We had friends from Great Harwood, near Blackburn, staying with at the farm for a week. As they were due to go home at the weekend and knowing that I had walks planned from Silverdale on the coming Saturday and Sunday, they asked if they could come along when I checked the sands and river crossing on the Friday. When I agreed everyone was so pleased and now, as well as Gordon and his daughter Barbara, there would be my daughter Jean and a very young Terry Austerfield (a relative of ours from Leeds), Mark Holden (Jean's friend at the time) and me. Six of us altogether and they were all feeling excited about going across with one whom they called 'Uncle Ced'. We took the train from Kents Bank station to Silverdale on a most beautiful sunny afternoon in August 1981.

When we left home I gave Olive the approximate times when to look out for us and a rough idea of how long it would take us to cross if all went well. I got quite a surprise after leaving the shore at Silverdale to come across large areas of quicksands and mud in the same area that only two weeks ago I had led several hundred walkers across. I was disappointed and now had to make back to the shore and take the road to Jenny Brown's Point.

As we passed Gibraltar Farm the views across the Bay were spectacular with the setting sun by now quite low in the west but looking like a massive great orange. The daylight had almost gone and stars were appearing in the sky by the time we had walked down to the Point and out on to the sands to see if it was a suitable place to start the forthcoming walks. It was still pleasant enough but starting to get a little overcast.

It seemed an age from leaving Jenny Brown's point to coming near to the River Kent but I was content in my mind now that I could start the walks from the Point. At first my small entourage were quite full of themselves and there were lots of questions asked, but now, as visibility became poor, everyone went quiet and kept very close to me. I knew the Kent pretty well from my daytime visits to the area but there was only one safe place to cross and every stride we took now brought us nearer to the river. We could hear fast running water, which sounded like rapids.

It was frightening for my followers, as by now it was becoming dark and the stars had disappeared behind newly formed clouds. I had to reassure them that I knew exactly where we were and that the noise was coming from what is called a gullet. This is where a fairly wide river suddenly narrows creating a very fast flow known as a gillimer. I told them we would have to go much higher before attempting to cross the river as by now it was really dark. After walking for a while I estimated that we were far enough away from the gullet to attempt our crossing. I led the way into the river, wading slowly, stick in hand and testing the surface as I went forward, with five people very close behind me.

There was no way that we could see to the other side, as by now it was just too dark. The depth was just under knee and we had gone about 150 yards when suddenly there was this huge brack, like a wall about ten feet tall. immediately in front of us. The sand under our feet was becoming softer, so I shouted for them to turn round and go back the way we had come. When the sands firmed up again under foot, I explained that with it being dark and us unable to see the course of the river, we had come higher up than we should have done. We slowly made our way down the river with the flow and, although this was pure guesswork with it being so dark, it brought us all together safely on the home stretch.

There were some sighs of relief. 'By gum, Uncle Ced, that was frightening,' came from young Terry. Gordon had a flashlight with him and thought he would keep shining it at intervals as we made our way towards Guide's Farm, leaving the eerie Kent well behind.

When we arrived back at the farm, Olive and Joan, Gordon's wife, had been worried sick. However, although we were a long way out of our estimated time, Olive knew that changes in the Bay can happen and things do not always go to plan. We all celebrated with a good meal and it was comforting just to sit there and listen to what they all had to say about this crossing of Morecambe Bay at night. Just a nightmare!

To Morecambe Bay...

I struggle to find the right words
When I speak of this magical place,
For I know when I wake, every morning
It will show me a different face.

Sometimes it looks grey and silver
Or at dawn there's a deep rosy hue:
The colours are constantly changing,
It's always a different view.

You can hear the call of the curlew,
See the heron, the geese and the gull.
It all depends on the season,
Whether the bay is empty or full.

The tide thunders in down the estuary
Churning the sands on its way
The bore can be seen from a distance
But it's not the same every day.

It casts a spell on the watcher
It invites you to linger and see
The rim of the hills in the distance
A place where the spirit is free.

It's simple and quite unaffected
But the grandeur is there to behold
Nothing could ever replace it
A place that's more precious than gold.

We have our own Guide, for the quicksands,
And his dignity matches this place.
His love for the Bay is unquestioned
And he leads with a consummate grace.

Its beauty is matched by the danger
Respect must always be shown.
How many have flouted the warnings
Will certainly never be known.

Once beguiled you will never escape it
But I'm willingly held in its sway,
I hope I may always live next to
The glorious sweep of the Bay.

Sue Wilkinson, Cart Lane

2. Life on Morecambe Bay
Fishing & Fishermen

Generations of Flookburgh families, together with other fishermen from surrounding villages, have earned their living from the sea and sands of Morecambe Bay. For many of the families working in the Bay, including our own, cockle fishing was the main source of our livelihood and there were hard times after the harsh winter frost of 1962-3. This decimated the cockle stocks and they did not begin to recover until the 1970s.

I have fished the Bay all of my life for cockles, shrimps, mussels, flukes and whitebait. Prices were often poor with very little return for all the hard work put in by the fishermen. The outlets for our fish - mainly cockles and shrimps - were the markets in the Lancashire and Yorkshire towns. Fishermen were getting more and more disheartened and began to think that they were being conned out of their payment, as 'condemned' notes came through their letter boxes from the wholesale fishmongers with increasing frequency. At that time there were about twenty-five fishermen in Flookburgh working the Bay from horses and carts. My ninety-nine year old father tells me that when he left school and started fishing with his father and his mother, there must have been at least one hundred fishermen and women with cockling and musseling being the main industry. There was no dole money in those days so they had to go fishing irrespective of whether they caught owt or nowt, because that was the only thing to do.

I have always enjoyed going out into the Bay from a very early age and have encountered all kinds of weather, but there is nothing nice about cockling in high winds that dry out the sands and make it difficult to use the jumbo board on the cockle beds. Our equipment had to be looked after out there with no shelter at all. I was shown as a lad that there was a right and wrong way to set the cockle basket and the riddle down on the sands without the strong wind sending them reeling for miles at such a speed you could never recover them.

When cockle beds are plentiful a combination of high tides and winds can move them quite long distances. They are usually brought to a halt by a build-up of sand or a dyke. When we found such cockles they were a welcome sight as they could usually be gathered without needing to use the jumbo.

Cockles to market
When our daughter Jean left school she followed the sands with me cockling, mostly through the winter months for the markets of Blackburn and Burnley. There were any amount of good quality cockles in Morecambe Bay but orders for them were few and far between as our markets were being flooded with imports from Holland at such low prices that it made it difficult to compete and make a living.

As Jean and I worked out on the sands cockling during the daytime, we would travel at night to arrive at the wholesalers about 3.30am. We always took a flask of coffee and a blanket with us as it became very cold sitting in the car if we arrived much earlier than anticipated and had to wait until they opened.

Our cockles were transported in a trailer towed behind my car. On one occasion we were driving along towards Blackburn after leaving the M6 motorway and thinking how good it was travelling through the night as we met so little traffic. Out of the blue the lights of a car showed in my mirror. As it approached the driver pulled alongside us, keeping parallel for quite a distance with the passenger glaring at me. I said to Jean, 'What are those silly so-and-so's up to?' Then suddenly they sped off in front of us and a sign lit up their rear window reading 'Police - Stop'. We did and the two plain-clothes men came to my driver's side as I opened the window. They asked me lots of questions, seemed satisfied that we were genuine and left us to continue our journey.

It was not always pleasant travelling at night as I can recall on our return journey home from Blackburn market to Grange. The rains came down like never before and we could hardly see the road in front of us. I did not have fixed rear lights on the car trailer so I had concocted some. A wooden pole fixed horizontally across the back with two bicycle rear lamps on either side looked pretty good when we set out from Grange. As we approached Forton Services on our return journey, the vibration on the way there must have loosened the rear lamps and they were now facing downwards with batteries running low!

A police patrol vehicle pulled us over with his bright flashing lights dazzling us in the horrible misty rain. The policeman was on his own and came towards us, then walked round to the back of our trailer. He came forward to me and said, 'Do you know that you have no rear lights on your trailer?' Then he asked me to step out of the car and take a look for myself.

He asked me lots of questions including details of where we lived. When I told him Grange-over-Sands and that I was born in Flookburgh he became interested and told me that he had friends there and gave me their names. I knew them well so now instead of 'going by the book' he advised me to pull into Forton Services and

spend time there until it became daylight instead of continuing our journey home and probably getting into more trouble. You can sometimes read a person by looking at them and this policeman had a good face and temperament to go with it. Jean and I thought that we had been very lucky as we sat over our cups of tea and looked across to a table. Chatting over a cuppa not far away from where we were sitting was a group of policemen, including the one whom had stopped us earlier.

The last time I delivered cockles to Blackburn market I vowed that I would never ever do so again by road. I was driving a van loaded with six hundredweight of cockles when it broke down close to the Blackburn turn-off from the M6. I managed to slip onto the hard shoulder just before the River Ribble. I saw lights across the fields so I left the old van and was frightened to death while crossing over the river as there was no hard shoulder and traffic was so close to me. I arrived at the Tickled Trout Hotel in the middle of the night and must have looked like a tramp. I had been cockling during the daytime, had not shaven and was wearing a long dark coat and my waders. A very polite young lady eventually appeared at the desk after I had been ringing the bell for some time.

I told her who I was, explained my predicament and asked if I could possibly use their phone. She not only allowed me to do so but also looked through the phone directory and then got through to my friend, Larry Bennett, a builder in Grange. I thanked her and made my way back towards the motorway, hoping that Larry would work something out. It was so cold and frosty that night as I sat in the van unable to keep warm. Suddenly the police arrived and gave me a good telling off, saying that I could not leave the vehicle there on the motorway and asking what arrangements I had made to have it removed. I told them that a friend was on his way to help me so they left me in peace.

It did not seem too long before Larry pulled onto the hard shoulder just behind me. He had brought along a large flask of coffee and we were just drinking the stuff (or was it nectar?) when another police car arrived and out jumped two of them. We explained what had happened and fortunately they were quite sociable.

Larry had just purchased a brand new Rover car and after we had drunk the coffee he put the seats down, spread out a cover and loaded the six hundredweight of cockles. Just imagine - how many people would subject their new car to this treatment? Larry attached a rope to the old van and towed it to a layby, where we unhitched it and drove on to Blackburn to deliver the cockles. On our return I jumped back into the van and Larry towed me all the way back to Grange. I shall never forget that night and what Larry and Christine, his wife, did for me. They are both truly remarkable friends.

Shellfish wars

Today full-time fishermen are few and far between and there is less than a handful working from Flookburgh. However, cockle beds have produced large quantities for the past three years and the local fishermen have had a bonanza, with cockles being in great demand all over Europe and fetching up to £400 per ton. When I was fishing the Bay for cockles, many a time they were so scarce that you had to work your butt off to make a living. Morecambe Bay covers such a large area that productive cockle beds can be miles apart. When you found a bed that was showing plenty of good-sized cockles you would keep it a secret as long as possible, even from other local fishermen.

There was concern in November 2002 when cocklers from the Dee estuary near Chester arrived in a large boat and anchored off the shore at Bare. In less than a week the number of fishermen had trebled and there were at least a hundred from Liverpool and North Wales going out from the promenade with rakes, buckets and netting. Some of them went zooming out across the mud on quad bikes to the cockle beds that were only a few hundred yards from the shore. The North West and North Wales Sea Fisheries Committee based at Lancaster University allowed

the boat to be used because the Dee estuary beds were closed and their cockles deemed unfit to eat because of algae poisoning, so they came and conquered but did have permission.

Shellfish wars are not new to the area. When I was a lad of ten I can remember travelling over to the Duddon estuary with dad and other Flookburgh fishermen to gather cockles from the Askam-in-Furness sands. The beds were close to the shore and the sand was much softer than it was in Morecambe Bay so there was no need to use the jumbo. We just raked them out of the soft muddy sand into a riddle and bagged them up. The local fishermen at that time were against us taking cockles from their shores but some of the Flookburgh men were hard cases and a match for anyone, so we did not come to any harm.

In February 1995 hundreds of cockle operators, not all fishermen, came in droves to take supplies from Morecambe Bay, working from Bardsea and Aldingham. These operators were from Liverpool, Morecambe, North Wales and Tyneside. Local fishermen along the coast road reacted bitterly to these offcomers and their actions, but the price of cockles was so high there was just no stopping them. Fights and rows erupted out there, as quad bikes and cocklers using tractors went into action.

Almost on the doorstep from where the cocklers were working, large beds of mussels had been banned for almost thirty years because of sewage outfalls. The shellfish were too contaminated to eat, but in 1993, when mussels were bringing £1,000 per ton, the European Commission lifted the total ban and allowed them to be taken for human consumption, providing they were put through tanks and purified or pre-cooked. The result was pandemonium. Hundreds of fishermen converged on the beaches to battle for rich pickings - and they did not even need a licence!

Searching for starfish

A type of fishing that was totally new to me and probably to Morecambe Bay was to gather starfish from the mussel scars not very far out from Heysham village. The starfish, which were about the size of a hand, had come in with the tide in their thousands and settled on the scars to feed on the mussels. The late John Foster of Grange asked if I would be interested in having a go at gathering them in for him. He told me that he had been onto the scars to have a look and thought it would be safe enough to work on them with my tractor.

I knew from earlier experience that this was not the case and to take a tractor on to the mussel scars would be asking for trouble. The sand on and around them may appear hard enough to the lay person but it contains a lot of clay. I needed the tractor to transport the starfish but left it a safe distance away. I then used a wheelbarrow to carry the fish-boxes and trays holding the starfish after they had been plucked from the mussel beds. I say 'plucked' because you could not just pick them up. They were under water, usually about knee deep, and had attached themselves to the mussels with a suction pad.

Picking starfish from the mussel beds made our hands very sore, as it was like handling sandpaper the whole of the time, so we decided to wear rubber gloves and these worked a treat. There was not a lot of time between tides to work on these beds, low down in the Bay, so it was essential to start collecting the starfish as soon as we knew the water had gone off the scars. We needed footwear for protection from the sharp mussel shells, with trousers and sleeves rolled up as far as we could get them, and then we would start 'plucking'. My son-in-law Chris worked on the scars with me until the starfish became hard to find.

While doing this work I noticed that an island appeared way out in the distance on the extreme tides, so I mentioned this to Larry Bennett, our good friend. Larry just loved a challenge and as Chris had already told him of the island, he suggested right away that he would come along with his four-wheel drive pick-up and with his small boat secured on a trailer to do a recce.

I went along with Larry and Chris the very next day as we drove around the Bay, through Morecambe and down to the little village of Heysham. From the square we took the narrow road down past several shops and the ancient St Patrick's Chapel on the left and out into the Bay. The sands journey from here was only a matter of minutes and when we arrived at a safe place to stop the three of us took the boat from the trailer and carried it to the water's edge. From here on I wanted nothing more to do with this expedition! Larry and Chris jumped into the flimsy small boat, put the oars in place and away they went out into the distance, with only a few inches showing above the water line. I stayed with Larry's vehicle and hoped for the best and their safe return.

They were quite pleased with themselves when they got back but not as pleased as I was to see them return safely. If the wind had struck up with the incoming tide, as it does many a time, they may just have been in trouble. The following day they left Grange in high spirits as they had found lots of starfish and were now on their way to sail out to the island in the sun. I was not happy about this as to sail all that way and put extra weight in that flimsy little boat was taking a big risk. They got simply loads of starfish and went back and forth sailing to the island over several days, but then the tides changed and it was covered with water until the next extreme tides.

The starfish were brought back to Guide's Farm where they were first washed and then stood in containers filled with fresh water to allow them to set in their natural shape. They were later taken out of the water and put into buckets containing formalin, then tightly sealed and sent to American universities for research purposes. Fishing for starfish was a very short season but it was different - and we three did enjoy ourselves out there in the Bay!

More on the fishing industry, the history and ecology of Morecambe Bay and historic images from the collections at Lancaster Maritime and Fleetwood museums can be found on: www.nettingthebay.org.uk

Search & Rescue

Morecambe Bay, for all its beauty, is still a dangerous environment and a danger to the unwary. Fast-running tides can cut you off from the safety of the shore, there is the dreaded fog and large areas of quicksands and mud that cannot be marked or mapped because of their frequent movements. At holiday resorts around the Bay and on the shoreline, notices are placed warning of the dangers, but occasionally people do wander out onto the sands and accidents happen. Normally those living locally are more careful but sadly this does not always apply.

In July 1987 I had a telephone call from the Lancashire Constabulary at Morecambe telling me that two teenagers were missing, presumed drowned on the treacherous sands. What had started out as a long-awaited seaside treat from a children's home ended in tragedy. A short while after arriving at a holiday caravan site the two excited young lads went out for a stroll and vanished in the fast incoming tide of the Bay. They had been told of the dangers of tidal currents, which have claimed many lives in the area out from Bolton-le-Sands, but they did not heed the warning.

When they failed to return that night a massive search operation got underway. Emergency services, including Arnside Inshore Rescue Team and mounted police, began a long and painstaking sweep of the coastline. At 8.45am on the Monday morning an RAF helicopter discovered the body of 16-year old Gary Thompson of Bilborough, Nottinghamshire. He was on the sands at Jenny Brown's Point, just south of Silverdale, some two miles up the Bay from where he had drowned.

A further extensive search in the area was carried out on the Monday and Tuesday, but no trace of 18-year old John Lindsay Thwaites of Beeston, Nottingham, could be found. Among the search and rescue teams were the distraught parents of the young lad, and the police advised them to come over to Guide's Farm and have a chat with me about the terrible tragedy. When they arrived I was out in the Bay fishing and Olive was on her own so she invited them in. When I returned, quite late that night, I cleaned myself up a bit and we all sat round the fireside with a cup of tea.

At first I felt very uneasy explaining to them how this could have happened. Although they were upset they were able to control their emotions, but what they could not understand was how their son had been drowned because he was such a superb swimmer with many medals to his name. I explained about the particularly high tides that had come into the Bay with such force. Previously the same area had been relatively safe, but with the River Kent changing its course to the Silverdale side it had now become dangerous with deep gullies and quicksands. These two poor young lads just did not stand a chance.

The parents did not want to leave the area until John's body had been found, so I suggested that they should stay over one more day. The police were in touch again at this stage asking for my advice on where to concentrate the search. With the tidal currents being known to me, I suggested that they now looked in one area only. This was the long seaward-facing wall out into the Bay from Jenny Brown's Point, which acts as a barrier against the incoming tide and was the most likely place to find the body. The next day he was spotted from a helicopter alongside the wall, partly covered with sand. If he had not been found on that tide, he might never have been seen again as he would have been buried under the sands. I received a letter of appreciation from the Chief Inspector of Police, Len Parry, for my assistance given during the search and recovery of the two young men.

In August 1996 Terry Howlett, a 29-year old from Darlington, left home for a night out in Carnforth, a place he used to visit when on leave from the navy. After deciding to walk out on the beach at Cote Stones near Warton, he realised he was in trouble when crossing a gully and his feet were sinking. The more he struggled the deeper he went up to his waist. Eventually he ceased sinking and the sand around him set like concrete. His shouts for help were not heard because of the wind and driving rain. How he survived the night is a miracle but the next morning a Mr Gardner fortunately heard his cries for help from his farm close to the shore. He called the police before seeking reinforcements. Fire, police and paramedics arrived, along with the Arnside Coastguards, but time was running short as the tide was well on its way in. By the time Terry Howlett was pulled clear the water was up to his neck and rising fast with some of the rescuers actually working below the surface. He was immediately airlifted by an RAF helicopter to the Royal Lancaster Infirmary suffering from hypothermia. Terry felt immensely grateful to the rescue teams who really did save his life - another ten minutes and he would have drowned.

A reconstruction of this incident was shown on the BBC TV '999' programme when the filming was done close to Morecambe Lodge Farm at Bolton-le-Sands. A stunt man was used, as they could not persuade Terry to repeat the performance! I was invited along as technical advisor for the making of the film, which was a quite different role for me but one I enjoyed to the full.

I think there will always be people who take it into their heads to wander out into the Bay regardless of all the warning signs, because there is no doubt that the sands do draw innocent people onto them. The recent deaths of Stewart Rushton and his son Adam on the sands off Bardsea have prompted a scheme for a rescue craft to be stationed in the Ulverston area but it is not yet known when this will be in operation. Hopefully, with more rescue services and with the up-to-date equipment available to them, they will provide a valuable safety cover on all parts of the Bay.

Morecambe Lifeboat

I am very grateful to John Beaty for this graphic account of the work done by Morecambe Lifeboat Station, which shows how vital it is to keep in touch with everyone to ensure safety. The crew certainly deserve the awards they have received for their role in rescues on the Bay:

"Due to the peculiar dangers of Morecambe Bay with its fast running tides and large areas of shallow water plus all-year-round boating activity, the lifeboat station was for many years one of the few ILBs (inshore lifeboats) to be in operation all year round and this distinction was a matter of pride to the station. All-year-round stations are common now, and it does involve the crews in some extremely cold and uncomfortable services during the winter months. With the introduction of one piece 'dry-suits' and 'polar suits by the Royal National Lifeboat Institute (RNLI), crew comfort and safety has been greatly enhanced.

In common with all other ILB stations, the work of the Morecambe ILB covers practically every aspect of saving life at sea: children trapped on rocks, people cut off by the tide on sandbanks, broken-down power boats, capsized dinghies, exhausted windsurfers, crashed aircraft, searches for missing boats, towing-in disabled fishing boats, even rescuing dogs and horses trapped on the marshes and on one occasion a deer. It can also be called on to assist the Coastguard and Fire Service in freeing people trapped in the quicksand which is common in some areas of the Bay.

Because of the ever-changing channels, the churlish tides and shallow waters, the ILB is practically the only type of craft that can respond to anyone in difficulties in the upper region of Morecambe Bay. Although at times it has to work to the upper limits of its capability.

In 1985 the station was one of four chosen to carry out exhaustive evaluation trials on the prototype of a new design of ILB. This prototype was given a thorough testing by the station crew under all weather conditions in company with the station boat so that a full comparison could be made. After the trials at Morecambe and the other stations involved, comments and recommendations were made and as a result, the RNLI introduced this new design into its fleet, gradually replacing the older ILBs as the new boats became available. Changes to new ILBs from 1997 included new all orange-coloured hulls.

In 1982 the Morecambe ILB was called upon by the police to carry out a service on the River Lune, where it runs through the centre of Lancaster. Two men had been swept down into a weir in the river when their light racing skiff had capsized in the strong currents. The boat had been swept and the two men had managed to hold onto a post on the weir in the middle of the river. The weather at the time was rather bad with a strong westerly wind, rain and very cold. To make the journey by sea from the boathouse to the men meant covering 19 miles of very rough water and would have taken about two hours in those conditions.

It was obvious that the two men could not survive long in the water so it was decided to take the lifeboat directly to Lancaster by road, a distance of only four miles. The police supplied a Land Rover to tow the boat, on its launching trolley, with two motorcycle outriders to clear the way. The lifeboat and escort left the boathouse, launched into the River Lune, picked up the two casualties and landed them into an ambulance all within fifteen minutes. The crew involved in this service all agreed that the most frightening part of the rescue was the road journey between Morecambe and Lancaster with the boat on its beach launching trolley, without breaks and suspensions, touching 50 m.p.h. down the main road.

The result of this service was the design and construction, by one of the crew, of a special road trailer that could be used at short notice to transport the lifeboat, complete with the launching trolley. This trailer was later replaced with one that can be used for transporting the boat by road or launching by a break back system. Since the first incident of road travel to Lancaster it has become standard practice to transport the ILB to the River Lune and Glasson Dock by road, many successful rescues being achieved in this way using the Land Rover which the RNLI issued to Morecambe station.

In April 1983 the station was visited by the Duke of Kent, president of the RNLI, and the chairman at the time, the Duke of Athol. The Duke of Kent revisited the station on 23rd July 2001 before opening Barrow's new station on 24th July.

Along with Hunstanton, Flint and West Kirby, Morecambe was chosen for trials of a new 7.6m (25ft) Griffon 450TD hovercraft, carried out for the two weeks beginning 24th July 2002. The trials were extremely successful at all stations and Morecambe was allocated the first one. A new Griffon 470TD was delivered on the 13th December 2002 and went into service on the 23rd December 2002.

The following awards have been made to the station:

1973 Bronze Medal
Two Bronze Medal Service Certificates

1981 Two letters of appreciation
Framed letter of thanks

1982 Silver Medal
The 'Maud Smith' award for the most courageous act of lifesaving

The 'Brewer' award
The 'Ralph Glistton' award for the most outstanding service by a lifeboat under 10 metres
Three Silver Medal Service Certificates

1983 The "Lifeboatman of the Year" award

1985 Two framed letters of appreciation

1990 Three 'Thanks of the Institution on Vellum'

2000 One 'Thanks of the Institution on Vellum'
Two framed letters of thanks

2003 RNLI inscribed binoculars

A secondary but important task that the Morecambe crew undertake is to visit the local schools giving talks to the children. Where possible the inshore lifeboat is taken to show the children. The equipment is demonstrated and the children are told of the dangers of the sea, getting stuck in quicksand and mud, and not to play at dodging the waves on the promenade. If the schools are too far from the lifeboat station to take the boat, the children are welcome to visit the station.

The station is well supported by a very active branch which, as well as undertaking the normal, never-ending thankless task of fund raising, also operate the souvenir shop at the boathouse and at events, such as church fetes, and also give talks to various organisations.

The first two call-outs for the newly commissioned ILB were false alarms. The first recorded effective service took place on the 3rd December 1966. A small boy, fishing with rod and line had got into difficulties 400 yards from the lifeboat station. When the ILB got to him the water was up to his knees and rising fast; he was picked up very cold, but no worse for his experience.

Some of the more unusual incidents include two youths getting into trouble after taking a boat with only one oar to rescue a boxer dog stranded on a sandbank. The lifeboat towed them back to shore, after picking up the dog and an exhausted seagull. This was the first of many calls to dogs in trouble that the ILB has been called on to assist.

On 25th August 1968 there was a report of a hydrofoil 150 yards off Morecambe promenade. It was eventually found three-quarters of a mile off Heysham harbour drifting rapidly west. It was safely recovered together with all the occupants.

Police reported an amphibious vehicle with four people on board bogged down in soft sand and the ILB stood by until it was able to float free. This incident on 16th July 1972 was the first of two calls to amphibious craft, the second on 19th June 1975 was not so lucky and could not be freed and sank. Fortunately there were no casualties.

The first of two calls to crashed aircraft was on the 12th December 1972. When the lifeboat reached the wreckage it was partly submerged and sadly the occupant had been killed on impact. A second call to an aircraft occurred on 10th August 1980 when the plane crash-landed on the shore at Morecambe and the three survivors were taken to hospital for check-ups but were not detained.

In 2002 the station was asked to assist with a deer which was on the beach at the west end of Morecambe. The boat was launched and the animal was found on a sandbank inshore. There was of course no possibility of the crew getting near to it and it was last seen heading off towards Grange-over-Sands having no trouble swimming the channels and is believed to have made it safely to the other side.

1st August 1974 saw a request to assist what was the largest craft ever for Morecambe Lifeboat. The Heysham Harbourmaster phoned the station's Honourary Secretary requesting help with a coaster that was bound for Lancaster and had missed the River Lune and sailed past Heysham Harbour and was heading for the shallows of Morecambe Bay. The ILB was launched to intercept before the vessel went aground. By the time the Lifeboat got to it the coaster was blithely steaming along a few hundred yards off Morecambe promenade in about a foot of water! The combined efforts of the ILB and local shrimp boats eventually persuaded the Master to put his ship about and head for the Irish Sea.

The above events are just a few of over 500 times that the Morecambe Bay Lifeboat had been alerted until the end of the year 2002. The others include the more common calls such as fishing boats, canoes, rowing boats, children and adults on airbeds, sailing and rubber dinghies, jet skis, people cut off by the tide, swimmers, attempted suicide and one or two regular customers who were, and some still are, on first-name terms with the crew."

Hovercraft on the Bay

In 1977 John Duerdon of Arnside Coastguard asked if I would be interested in joining their Auxiliary Service reporting station. I readily agreed and was officially enrolled. I am still an Auxiliary Coastguard and have watched with great interest a recent development that is a huge asset in safety terms. Stuart Hamilton, secretary and treasurer of Bay Hovercraft Rescue, takes up the story:

"In 1996 the Coastguard Team of Arnside received an emergency call to attend a man who had been stuck in the quicksand out on the Bay for almost ten hours. He had walked out on a part of the sands not easily observed from the shore and had found himself stuck, and then sinking, in a very wet and dangerous piece of quicksand. His cries for help had gone unheard for many hours, during which time he had sunk in up to his chest, and he was aware that the tide must soon be on its way in.

Arnside Coastguard is probably one of the most experienced mud and quicksand teams in the UK, but this rescue was to prove to be a race against time in which they, and their rescue equipment, had to travel a considerable distance from their base and the shore-line to attend to the casualty whose life was in imminent danger. Indeed, the tide was already running in before they were able to extricate him by the use of 'water-lances', which force water down the sides of the legs, and in this case the body of the trapped person in order to loosen the sand and free that person. Not only was the man at grave risk, but throughout the rescue operation the coastguards themselves were struggling to ensure they too did not also become stuck.

Two of the Auxiliary Coastguards involved in this rescue, Gary Parsons and Adrian Swenson, decided that there must be more effective ways

not only to transport rescue equipment across the sands (where even the most robust four-wheel drive vehicle would become quickly stuck), but also transport a rescue crew to people who, if not trapped in quicksand, could be at risk of being caught by the fast flowing incoming tide. Arnside Coastguard has a rib-craft that is invaluable when the tide is in but, as with most large estuaries, for large parts of the time there is little or no water in Morecambe Bay except in the narrow channel formed by the River Kent. If you cannot use the rescue boat then basically you have to walk out to the casualty or person(s) in trouble.

Gary and Adrian agreed that a hovercraft could be the ideal solution to enable the rescue crew and equipment to be taken out across sand and water without fear of the craft becoming stuck. A hovercraft would also be quick and would not be affected should the tide be coming in or going out: it would simply 'float' from one surface to another.

From several discussions about the logistics of using a hovercraft (which incidentally neither the Coastguard or RNLI had any official view or intention to utilise as rescue craft at that time), Gary Parsons bought himself an ex-formula one hovercraft to 'see how one performed' over all the hazardous and potentially lethal shifting sands. After many outings on a huge learning curve to become proficient at 'flying' his craft, and finding out how you can crash one too, Gary was now absolutely convinced that a search and rescue hovercraft based in the bay could and would prove to be a valuable life saving asset.

His logic was that if someone was stuck in or on the sands and more than a few metres from the shore (and some people do get themselves into trouble well away from easy access from the more popular parts of the shore) and the tide was due in, then time was to be of the essence for the rescue team. A hovercraft could both search and provide assistance and rescue very quickly, and go where no other vehicle could go. It would also take rescuers and their equipment, and thereby save long and sometimes hazardous walks across the sands. For search purposes, vast areas and distances can be covered in a way that only a helicopter could, but a hovercraft would be much cheaper.

Now a single-seater ex-racing hovercraft does not meet the specification for search and rescue purposes. Gary and Adrian began to research what sorts of craft were available, what they cost and so forth. Through various connections, both in the Coastguard and mountain rescue teams, they were put in touch with a wealthy local benefactor who was noted for her immense generosity towards mountain rescue teams in the Lake District and to the RAF helicopter teams from Boulmer in Northumbria. Discussions followed. It turned out that the lady in question had experience of the perils of Morecambe Bay many years ago when her then young son had become trapped in quicksands. His rescue had been traumatic and she completely understood the proposal put to her by Gary and Adrian about the value of using a hovercraft on the Bay for search and rescue purposes.

As a result a cheque was handed over to what had then become the beginnings of Bay Hovercraft Rescue, or BHR as the team refers to it. In June 2001 Bay Hovercraft Rescue took delivery of a brand new Osprey 5, mark 2 hovercraft. But this is to jump ahead of some key events.

With a promise of substantial funds to purchase a craft and trailer on which to transport it, came the issue of where to base it. Using their knowledge of the Bay, Gary and Adrian began to look for a site from which to base the operations of the craft. Arnside was a possibility as a suitable launch site, but there was nowhere immediately suitable to house the craft. Other

potential sites were looked at. A discussion with Cedric Robinson was to prove to provide the answer. He advised Gary and Adrian that they should approach Tim Rogers, the manager of the Abbot Hall Hotel at Kents Bank, where there was a very large and only partly used garage (an old wartime fire station) which could be suitable. It was also only a hundred yards from the shore, which is accessed down a lane and across the railway line onto a perfect launching slipway. Cedric had already 'put a word in' by the time Gary and Adrian approached the hotel. The Abbot Hall Hotel is part of the Christian Guild Holiday Centres. Tim Rogers, the then manager, was only too pleased to offer 'garage space' to BHR and from there on BHR was in business.

In August 2001, following initial trials of the craft in various parts of the Bay and from a farm near Leven, where the River Kent outfalls into the Bay, BHR had its formal public launch at an event at Abbot Hall. The craft was officially named Lady Ada, after our benefactor Mrs H, by Lord Cavendish of Furness. The event, on a rather cold and wet day, was attended by members of Coastguard teams from all around the Bay and many members of the public from Grange. By this time BHR had increased its membership and this event brought more local volunteers on board.

The official launch was one thing but BHR was not yet ready to be operational as an 'additional facility', that is to be a resource to be called upon by the Coastguard and other emergency services. The craft had several teething problems to be sorted out. Pilots had to be trained and various pieces of equipment, such as hand-held VHF radios, were required. The major stumbling block, however, came down to insurance. Public Liability Insurance is an absolute necessity in this day and age. Finding an insurance company to provide cover seemed to be impossible. No one had ever set up a search and rescue operation using a hovercraft in the UK before. Underwriters did not want the business, or if they did they wanted many thousands of pounds for minimal cover.

Without insurance (and we had no problem covering it for theft and fire!), training pilots and crew was not possible in a public area. Arguably, there's less chance of running someone over in the middle of the Bay than there is of having an accident in a car in the middle of Grange, but BHR couldn't take the risk. It took several months of many phone calls and lengthy searches on the Internet before we made contact with a shipping insurer in Kent. If funding and Abbot Hall had been the first two 'miracles', then Everards was the third. Insurance was secured, not cheaply but at a reasonable cost for good cover.

Local support for BHR has been brilliant with funds and donations coming from a wide range of sources. In November 2001 BHR registered as a company and in February 2002 it gained status as a registered charity.

A great deal of time, effort and hard work has gone into forming BHR and getting it to a point whereby operational cover is available during evenings and weekends. Continuous cover is some way off, but tremendous progress has been made and we strive to improve and develop. BHR received its first call out from the Coastguard in late July 2002 and the craft was launched to attend an incident beyond the viaduct at Arnside. Once launched at Kents Bank, it literally takes eight minutes to cross the Bay (somewhat quicker than a crossing with Cedric on foot) and about twelve minutes to get under the viaduct. The incident, involving a sailing dinghy and a distraught owner was dealt with swiftly and safely. The craft and its crew had to negotiate both tidal channels and dangerous areas of sands to carry out this rescue but it proved the point that a hovercraft was the only vehicle that could have done this.

Shortly after this BHR took ownership of two all-terrain vehicles called Argos. These vehicles are about ten feet long, four feet six inches wide, have eight-wheel drive, carry up to six people, and are semi-amphibious. Used widely on the Scottish shooting estates, and in Canada from where they originate, the Argos were seen as

filling the final gap in additional safety provisions on the Bay. The Coastguard's rib-craft meets the requirements for rescues when the tide is in or running on a big tide. The hovercraft can cross the sands very quickly and virtually go anywhere on sand or water (as long as the latter is not excessively rough) in the Bay and can provide safety cover for the many cross-Bay walks that Cedric leads.

However, anyone familiar with the 'spartina problem' off the front of Grange and other parts of the Bay will understand that a hovercraft will have some difficulties flying over the rough spartina and the hidden channels that run through it. Quite simply the craft loses too much air from its cushion due to the rigidity of the grass for it to fly effectively. The Argos were bought to ensure that no part of the Bay is not accessible to search and rescue teams. They have no problem in negotiating this rapidly expanding colonised shore area.

Such is their flexibility as rescue vehicles that they can cover the shore and grass areas whilst the hovercraft covers all the sands beyond. The Argos are available to local mountain and fell rescue teams to provide logistical support to their operations. They also climb up very steep hills!

Bay Hovercroft Rescue has come a very long way since Gary and Adrian first thought about using a hovercraft as a search and rescue vehicle. The resources of BHR have increased considerably and the team is developing its skills and knowledge. We have learned a great deal, both about flying a thing that has no brakes and feels like driving a car on ice, and about the Bay and how it constantly changes. We are all much more aware of what a perilous place it can be for the unwary."

(Opposite) Hovercraft are now regarded as invaluable in rescuing people stuck in or on the sands, as they can search and provide assistance very quickly indeed. Able to go almost anywhere on land or water, they can reach areas that a conventional craft or vehicle would find impossible. Here a hovercraft is seen in action on the shore of the Bay (top), together with a close-up of Cedric being given a demonstration by its crew (below).

Birds of the Bay

Morecambe Bay is an amazing place. It is the second largest bay in Great Britain and is a haven for some 150 different species of sea birds. That number amazes me and I must admit that I could not name them all, but on my travels across the sands I see large numbers, mainly gulls, terns, shelduck, dunlin and oystercatcher.

The common tern resembles the gull but is much smaller, and is grey and white with a forked tail. They usually come into the Bay about April and stay until October. When the tide is in they can be seen not very far out from the shore, diving for small whitebait to take back to their nests to feed their young. I often see them in large numbers in stretches of shallow water, feeding on small shrimps when they are close together. They make such a noise that they do not seem to notice my tractor engine and I am able to drive in quite close without them taking flight.

I have not seen dunlin in the Bay in the same large numbers as in the last two years. These small but fascinating birds are a wonder to watch and you just cannot take your eyes off them. As they fly past on the sands, and many a time when I have been out there setting my fluke net, I suddenly hear the sound of wings and then they are gone, wheeling and turning with the mass of birds forming a cloud that forever changes shape. They are so beautiful to watch as they turn in the sunlight, their colour changing to light, then to shade. When they do settle down on the sand to feed their movements are so quick and they run just like mice. That is why Flookburgh fisherman - including myself - call them 'sea mice'.

Large flocks of colourful shelduck (the local name for this bird is 'skelly') spend hours out there in the Bay shovelling and siphoning the softer and wet areas of sand for food. In the mating season these birds can be seen inland, male chasing female on the ground, and when in flight they make such a noise.

The sheltered shores and islands provide these birds with safe nesting places, which are often in rabbit holes. When the eggs have been hatched the young are very soon able to walk, following behind the mother almost like little humbugs on legs and making their way to the shore and into the Bay. This is the most dangerous part of their early lives. If they get separated from the mother, then the drake is close by and he is the 'childminder' always on the lookout for danger.

Local fishermen regularly come across groups of shelduck with their young and keep well clear, but now and again you encounter them unawares and get too near. The drake will immediately fly close to you, skimming the surface of the sand and sometimes dropping a wing as if wounded. This move is to take your attention away from the young ones. If they were to get split up the gulls are always waiting for any undefended chicks and, very sadly, they will pick them off like ninepins and fly away with them.

The most common of the large waders to be seen in the Bay is the oystercatcher, nicknamed the 'sea-a-pie', with its black and white plumage and orange bill. Their food consists of a wider variety than most of the waders, though cockles are their favourite and there has been no shortage of these during the past three years. They also feed on mussels as they can prise the shells open with those long, pointed and powerful beaks. Young mussels are called spat and settle on the stony scars off Morecambe, Heysham, Rampside, Knott End and Fleetwood during the late winter and early spring. This is food for the smaller birds such as dunlin and knott.

Welcome visitors to the Grange shore and noticeably in the same area for the last three years have been large numbers of up to two hundred or so greylags and pink-footed geese. They arrive from the north for the winter and gather to feed on the lush marsh grass that now seems well established and is taking over from the very unpopular spartina. I think I can speak for most of the residents in Cart Lane when I say it is a pleasure to see and hear them out there, feeding when the tide is out and so close to the shore. The downside of this is that wildfowlers have found easy pickings and come down to Cart Lane and out onto the sands to shoot them. They usually arrive at the edge of dark or at dawn when the birds are settled and not in flight. The Bay would not be the same without the wildfowl, so why are they not protected like other birds?

Another sight worth seeing is the cormorants and shag. I love to watch them on the edge of the River Kent in summer fishing for flounders. From a distance these quite large dark-coloured birds can be mistaken for small groups of people and it is only when they decide to spread their wings and stay put that they are recognised. At one time there was a price on their heads because of the quantity of fish they needed to survive, but nowadays they come to no harm and it is so nice to see them out there at nature's best.

COMMON SHELD-DUCK.

DUNLIN.

STORM PETREL.

CORMORANT.

OYSTER CATCHER.

G. Robinson.

LESSER BLACK-BACK GULL.

(This page) *Gathering cockles out on the sands by traditional methods. Although the cockle beds were decimated in the harsh winter of 1962-3, they began to recover in the 1970s and local fishermen have recently enjoyed a bonanza. Cockles are now in great demand all over Europe and have been fetching more than £400 per ton. (Tom Stephen - 2)*

(Opposite) *Seen against one of the famous 'big skies' of Morecambe Bay is The Sandpiper, a trailer converted to offer two-hour trips out onto the sands. They became extremely popular, one lover of fast cars commenting that it had been his 'most interesting ride of the year'! Cedric is demonstrating how the jumbo board is used to bring cockles to the surface, as can also be seen in the top photograph opposite. (Gary Taylor)*

The Sandpiper

No - it is not a bird but a trailer! It is pulled by my Leyland diesel tractor and has slatted wooden seats down the centre with cushions and blankets provided plus a roof over your head - that's about it. Larry Bennett had the idea several years ago and promptly set about and built the Sandpiper.

Fishing had been on a downward trend for some years so this was going to be an entirely new venture that I was willing to try. Holidaymakers coming to Grange and Kents Bank seemed to like the idea of a two-hour ride out into the Bay and back. Many passengers could not have managed to walk the sands as they were quite elderly, so they thought it was a wonderful opportunity to be able to go out into the heart of the Bay - often for the first time in their lives.

Access from the shore at Kents Bank onto the sands was quite muddy and through daily following the same route it eventually became impossible for Sandpiper and my tractor. Then a wonderful opportunity arose as I drove towards the railway crossing at the station. Men and machinery were everywhere starting work on the platforms and what they were digging up - the old tarmac surfaces - was just the kind of rubble I had been seeking. There is a saying, 'it always comes to those who wait', and this proved true as the material could not have been handier. The workers offered to transport it down on to the shore at the bottom of the ramp where my nephew Kenny and I loaded the backboard of my tractor. We laid some huge pieces in the ruts on the track and eventually the route became hard but rather bumpy.

There was a lot to see and talk about on the Sandpiper trips. On neap tides and given fine weather, the sand dried out on the higher sandbanks for miles, so after a journey of about three-quarters of an hour I would halt the tractor and give passengers a choice. Some wanted to leave the Sandpiper and have a walk on the sands, sometimes barefooted if the weather allowed. Others preferred to chat with one another, take photographs and ask lots of questions.

I could vary the route, but ideally it was best to travel down into the heart of the Bay first and have a good look around. On the return journey I would go over towards Humphrey Head. If there were ample time I would take the Sandpiper around the west side so that the passengers could disembark and have a look at the 'holy well' of St Agnes. I would also read out the inscription on a limestone slab commemorating William Pedder, an unlucky youngster who lost his life climbing up the face.

There was only one snag with these rides out onto the sands and that was the absence of toilet facilities. You had to make sure of a visit before embarking on the venture. Most people could manage for about two hours or so, but I do remember one occasion when we came towards Humphrey Head and a point where I stopped close to the rocks so that passengers could look out for fossils. As I jumped from the cab of the tractor and walked back to talk to the group, a man sitting on the seat alongside his wife beckoned me as if he wanted to tell me something. He whispered into my ear, 'Mr Robinson, my wife is feeling sick, could you kindly let us off the Sandpiper?'

I obliged and she immediately grabbed me by the arm and made for the rocks, but the poor woman could hold out no longer - up with her dress, down with her knickers and that was it! I do not know who was the most embarrassed - the woman or her husband or me. Nothing was said as she straightened her dress and then stepped back into the Sandpiper. I fastened the safety bar across the back and we made our way back across the sands to the shore at Kents Bank. This was a one-off unfortunate incident, but now that South Lakeland District Council has decided to close the toilets at the station it could become to be a regular occurrence.

When we arrived back safely at Kents Bank the passengers always commented on their trip. One gentleman and justice of the peace, Roy Brooks from Bury, wrote me a letter when he got home from his holiday saying how much he had enjoyed going out into the Bay. One of his great joys in life was to drive large and powerful cars, the more luxurious the better and preferably on a long, fast run. It had therefore come as a total surprise on the last day of his 1990 holiday to

have what he regarded as the most interesting ride of the year. Moreover, this was in a vehicle that went only at walking pace, had little more brake horse power than a Mini and provided less comfort than a park bench. His letter concluded: 'The venue was the notoriously treacherous sands of Morecambe Bay, but the driver and "Sand Pilot" was none other than the Official Queen's Guide, Cedric Robinson, who has spent a lifetime in his unique profession.'

Occasionally the Sandpiper went through water deep enough for a small boat to sail in, and sometimes the mud was up to the axles, but the four-cylinder diesel never missed a beat. For all that took part in this one-off water trip, it was an exhilarating experience. A word of warning though, even if you have a four-wheel drive vehicle do not be tempted to have a go yourself. What looks perfectly solid can all too easily be anything but firm, and what may be an excellent route one day can be totally different the next.

(Opposite, top) Horses have always played a prominent role in life at Guide's Farm, especially in the period when Cedric's daughter Jean was 'pony mad'. This more recent view shows 'Chester' in 2001. (Paul Nickson)

(Lower) Eight years earlier, Cedric is seen with 'Domino' in July 1993. (David C Pearson)

(This page) Haytime at Guide's Farm, a smallholding with ten acres of good land and what must be one of the world's finest views from a meadow. Cedric and Olive became virtually self-sufficient through rearing their own stock, growing vegetables, keeping hens to lay eggs and catching fluke from the Bay. They even supplied orders to local railwaymen, who - unseen by authority -would stop their trains outside the front door! (Gary Taylor)

3. Guide's Farm - and beyond

Work and more work

When we moved to Guide's Farm in October 1963 we found we had a lot to do to make ourselves comfortable. Everyone was willing to help and work day and night if necessary, as this was my busiest time on the sands.

Fishing was my livelihood, with shrimping in full sway. I kept my tractor and fishing gear on my parents' land in Flookburgh as there was no access onto the sands at Cart Lane or Kents Bank station owing to the River Kent then running close to the rocky shore. Having progressed from the horse and cart era into the tractor age, the long weary journeys in all weathers were now almost halved.

Trawling for shrimps in the Bay is only the start, as most of the work with inshore fishermen begins when you arrive home. To make it easier for Olive I would lay the fire, sticks and coal to heat the boiler, and give her an idea of the time when Bill and I would return with our catch. This helped as she lit the fire in readiness and the shrimps could then be put straight into the boiler. They were later spread out on trays to cool, riddled and were ready for shelling - known locally as 'picking'.

Guide's Farm was always a busy but happy house. At weekends and during school holidays we would be full of children all sitting around a large table in the centre of the room picking shrimps. They were a good help and could earn a little money for themselves. Olive was good at picking as were all members of our family. There were other very good pickers in Ravenstown and Cark as well as Flookburgh so some of the shrimps were sent out to various households in buckets and then collected later the same day

It was quite common at Guide's Farm to see people sat round the living room table picking away until late at night. After everyone had gone home, Olive would set about to clean and wash down. We had oilcloth on the table and linoleum on the floors as coconut matting was a luxury.

Shrimping went on from March till the first signs of frosts, usually about October into November, and if these were severe for a few nights in succession it brought the season to an abrupt end. If there was no shrimping and no cockles were to be found in the Bay, we were kept very busy making holly wreaths and crosses for Christmas, which my parents sold on Barrow-in-Furness outdoor market. We made hundreds of them and it was hard work, so much so that Olive's fingers became septic with the constant pressing and bending of the wires through the moss and holly. She never grumbled, although it did take them a while to heal properly.

There was very little time to prepare for Christmas but Olive always made the living room cosy and warm and it was a happy time for us. There was a lovely big open fire and a Christmas tree in the corner of the room. There were no lights - only two lamps that hung down from the large beams - but we had lots of decorations and so many Christmas cards.

It was usual when the family had gone up to bed on Christmas Eve for Olive to leave a glass of wine and a carrot on the hearth - the wine for Father Christmas and the carrot for his reindeer! The next morning there were large red socks hanging up at either side of the fireplace full of all sorts including oranges, apples, nuts and presents that Father Christmas had delivered down the chimney. Everyone was so happy that the wine had been drunk, the reindeer had eaten the carrot and Father Christmas had left the children lots of toys and gifts.

The winter seemed long and we were looking forward to the day when we could have electricity brought to the house. We had been using oil lamps and candles for almost six months - although it seemed much longer. After applying to the Electricity Board things soon got moving and in February 1964 the work was finished and the current was turned on. This changed all our lives, but none more so than that of Olive.

When no cockles were to be found in the Bay we had long winter months without any money to be made. Things got desperate so I took a job along with a fishing pal of mine, Brian Shaw, at a factory in Barrow-in-Furness known as Listers, where we were each put in charge of a loom. The noise was terrible. Neither of us had clocked in for a job before in our lives - but here we were, desperate to have a go. It was so warm in the factory that we wore only what was essential, with no shirt and just a vest, trousers and carpet slippers. No one, except the supervisor, ever spoke a word to either of us. It was as if we had some sort of infectious disease! I stuck it out for only two weeks and was out of there like a shot. As bad as things were on the sands, this was not a job for me.

An opportunity arose to work on the site of the new Heysham Power station. A local character, George Broadhurst, had a contract with a firm digging trenches and laying electricity cables and he was looking for labourers. I joined his team of local lads and we used to pick George up at Cartmel in the early morning and arrive at Heysham just as it was getting light.

This was winter time and nearly every morning we would grab our picks and shovels, jump into a trench with snow and ice still around and work like navvies. When the weather eventually broke down and the rains came, every worker except our gang would go under cover. After a while other men on the site approached George asking him if we were in the union. His reply was, 'The only union we will be joining is the Mothers' Union and you can go to hell!' Not long after it was decided that if we did not join we would be out of a job. We joined. However, when spring arrived I decided to give in my notice as it was time to start fishing again.

In the early 1960s I was involved in the Morecambe Bay Barrage Survey, which proved to be a very interesting and rewarding two years. Olive and I made lots of new friends. One of them, a very generous man called 'Big Frank', was in charge of drilling in the Bay. When the tides were unsuitable or at weekends, he would turn up with something or other. He just loved his food but always wanted to share it with others. Generally we would have just finished our meal when Frank arrived carrying two shopping bags that usually contained liver, bacon, sausages and lamb or pork chops. There was enough to last for weeks but Olive would start cooking all over again and put these under the grill to please Frank. I think that I put on more weight in those two years than at any other time. We did keep in touch for a while, but I heard not long ago that 'Big Frank' had passed away.

From the family album.

(This page, top) *Shelling shrimps - - known locally as 'picking' - about 1981. From left to right are Olive, daughter Jean, John Shaw and Cedric. All the Robinson family are good 'pickers' and would often sit round the living room table shelling away until late at night. (Paul Nickson)*

(Opposite) *Cedric and Olive, framed by the front doorway of Guide's Farm. (Peter Thompson)*

Farm enterprise

There is very little payment from the Duchy for my services as Guide - £15 per year - but Guide's Farm is a smallholding with some ten acres of good land, so I wrote to the trustees and got permission to cultivate the part behind the house. As I already had a Ferguson tractor and the implements for ploughing and the like, we could now grow our own vegetables, catch flukes from the Bay, have fresh eggs from our own few hens that we had recently purchased and be almost self-sufficient. In summer we put a sign outside the garden gate reading 'Fresh Fish for Sale'. I always filleted the flukes and my - were they good, beating your expensive plaice every time!

The railway runs past the house on an embankment and the drivers of steam trains, both passenger and goods, would stop on the run towards Barrow, jump down from the train and come to the wall to shout out their orders. They asked either Olive or myself what was available, so we would have the fish wrapped ready for them on their return. These were very good orders as the drivers who came from Carnforth had not tasted fluke for years, so they were really glad of them and we at the farm were thankful for their custom.

We next had the idea of buying some young cattle from the farm sales as they would keep the grass down and could be sold on as two-year olds. Bill, our eldest son, was very keen so we went ahead and things went well at first, even though it was a case of trial and error. We bought a suckler cow, on advice from a local farmer, and bred a jolly good calf from it. The mother was tied in a stall with the cowband and the calf was allowed to run loose and suckle when it felt like it. Unfortunately the calf got its head into a bin where we kept the barley to feed the mother, bloated itself and died. This was a lesson we learnt the hard way.

Calves were much smaller forty years ago and when purchased from farm sales were put in hessian sacks with just their heads sticking out. They were then brought home in the back of the van. It is different today with most continental breeds being much bigger at birth so there is just no way you would be able to transport them in this manner.

I purchased two wooden poultry houses, one of them on wheels, from Mike and Henry Garnett and put them halfway up the paddock. The idea was to rear turkeys, buying them at six weeks old and getting them ready in time to sell for Christmas. These were large turkey whites that grew to tremendous sizes. They were kept inside at first and when old enough they ran free range but were always fastened up at night on account of foxes. Bill and I were late back from the sands one night and when we went up to the paddock to lock up the turkeys we noticed that six were missing. As we walked through the meadow towards the big ash tree the six turkeys were perched quite high up, so we both thought they would be safe until the morning. Not so, as very early I walked through the meadow and found them with their heads off, killed by a fox.

I was so annoyed that I decided to lay in wait for it the next morning. Just before daylight my son Robert and I walked up the paddock and found a secluded spot near an old well, camouflaged with bushes all around us. It was a wet and very quiet, misty morning as we sat hidden with a shotgun. We did not have to wait long before the weirdest barking began. I had never heard a fox bark before, and this seemed so loud I thought everyone in Grange would be wakened.

The fox could be heard coming towards us and passed not too far away but it was not light enough to see it. We both sat there till daylight and then Robert had to be in Grange for work at 7.30am so we left our hideout and headed up the field. Suddenly we saw Master Reynard heading back but well out of range. Perhaps this was just as well as neither of us had shot at anything before! He had been on his rounds and was probably looking for the turkeys he had killed the night before, but he was unlucky this time.

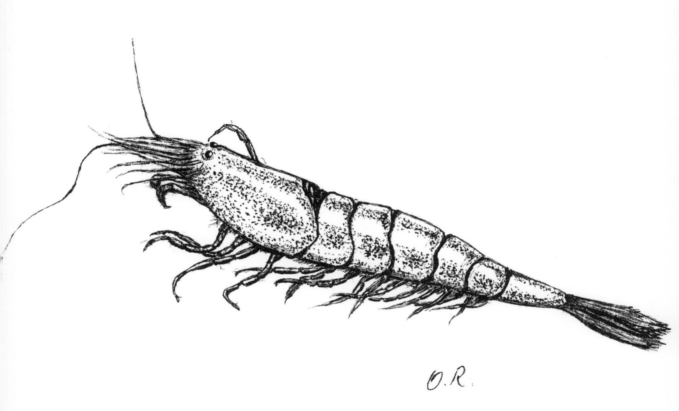

O.R.

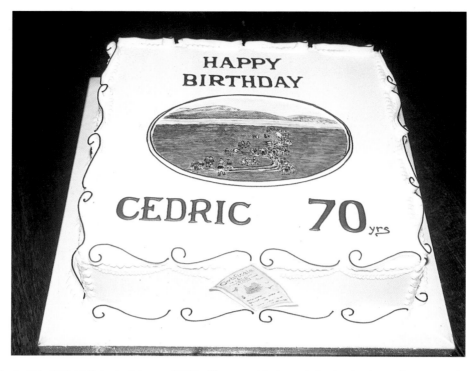

Cedric celebrated his 70th birthday in February 2003 with a superbly decorated cake showing walkers streaming out into the Bay. (Paul Nickson)

To Ced

You are seventy years of age
Have written many a page
For forty years the guide
You've done your job with pride
An exciting life it's been
You even met the Queen
We are thinking of you
and of Olive too
So have a lovely day
HAPPY BIRTHDAY

Gordon Cilgram

With all good wishes and our love
Gordon, Joan & Barbara

"Summat in that water"

When fishing was poor and no money was to be made on the sands, my father found work on local farms, either thinning turnips, muck spreading, haytiming or draining the land. One day he was asked by Jimmy Edgar, who farmed Field Head at Flookburgh, if he would look at a wet area in the paddock in front of the house and check the land drains. Dad told me that as long as he could remember that field had always had a 'dub' - a waterlogged area with rushes growing around it. When he dug to find the old drains, the one in question was running at full bore all the time so he put it back just as it was and told Jimmy that it must be a natural spring.

Nothing more was thought about the spring until after dad had bought our horse from Harry Shaw, a fisherman in the village. She was a chestnut mare standing about sixteen hands high and had a very quiet nature. She was good on the sands and in the water shrimping but had a mild form of illness that the local veterinary surgeon could not recognise so she was never treated.

Grazing land was difficult to obtain after the war, so we stabled the horse and scythed the grass verges every few days. This was hard work and inconvenient, but then we were lucky and were able to rent a small paddock that had been taken over by the War Ministry. After we had put the horse in this paddock, which was an extension of the dub field with the spring water, we noticed in a matter of weeks that she became more sprightly and was a different animal. There was very little grass for her to eat but an endless supply of water.

Years later, when we had moved into Guide's Farm and our daughter Jean had left school, we owned several ponies as she and all her friends were 'pony mad'. Among them was a lovely but aged gelding we called Flash and he was not doing too well. We always had plenty of help with the ponies from eager youngsters, boys as well as girls. Gary Lynott used to come along from Flookburgh and now and again went out onto the sands with me to fish the fluke nets. Gary mentioned to his dad, Philip, that one of our ponies was not doing as well as it should have been, so Phil suggested that I should take it over to his place and put it in his paddock to see how it fared. It was the paddock with the dub in it - and the change was amazing.

I went along with dad about a fortnight later and we were leaning over the gate looking at our pony, when Phil spotted us and came down for a chat. The pony had had its head down for quite some time in the same spot and dad wondered what was up. We opened the gate and all three of us went over towards Flash. As it lifted its head, water dribbled from its mouth. Then all of a sudden it shot off round the paddock at full gallop, like a two-year old. Dad said, 'Well I nivver, there must be summat in that watter that's done him some good.'

Phil was so pleased to see such a change in Flash in so short a time. He later bought two ponies himself and stabled them because of their poor condition. Both of them had got strangles, a terrible illness that meant their throats had swelled and they had a nasal discharge. Spring came along and Phil took a chance by turning them out to grass in the paddock with the dub. There was very little for them to eat but after just a few days there was a remarkable improvement.

Many years later Phil decided that he would like to know more about the spring on his land, so he went along to see my father. Dad has a remarkable memory and was able to show him the exact spot where the drain carrying the water could be found. Phil dug down, bricked round the spring and put in a manhole nearby. He kindly allowed me - and I believe dozens of other people - to take the water home and try it for ourselves.

Three years ago Phil, David Jones and Ian Needham gathered around the spring and decided to do something about it. A pump was installed and one of the most up-to-date bottling plants in the country built, so that the wonderful Lakeland Willow Spring Water can now be appreciated nation-wide.

When I told dad about this, he said jokingly, 'Aye, an' 'ad it nut bin for me, they wud nivver 'ad fund it, so I should have a share in it, shouldn't I?'

'No,' he added, 'I wish 'em well and the best of luck with it. If tha sis 'im, tell 'im waint ta.'

I certainly did, and at a later date Phil gave me a tour of the new factory and bottling plant - and plenty of bottled water to keep us going for some while. Good luck, Phil!

Champion dogs

Most of our time at Guide's Farm is taken up with our work and we have never really thought about or had any time for hobbies, or even a short-break holiday. One day on a visit to Silverdale we came across a man with several little dogs and they were the most beautiful we had ever seen. Chihuahuas of all colours but mostly light cream, some were long-coated and others very tiny and smooth-coated. Olive and me were invited back to his home and given lots of doggy information. We had always had a terrier or greyhound, but now I thought I would like to buy Olive a small dog.

We had heard of a well-known breeder at Braintree in Essex and we eventually bought a little gem of a dog from him. He came by rail in a carrying case in the very good care of the guard, who had promised to give him water and look after him on the long journey. I met the train at Grange station. He was a lovely red-coloured long-coat with white markings and we decided to call him Chico.

There were more to come of these little dogs so full of character and we now had a hobby that enabled us to get away from work for a while. Olive started showing them with pride and great success and would come away from shows with many prizes. It was good entering the dogs at agricultural shows in the summer, where most of the people knew each other and really enjoyed the day out. At large shows the competition was always much fiercer but Olive did well. She even made it to Crufts, which was definitely an experience! As she became better known as an exhibitor, she was also invited to judge her little favourites on many occasions.

One day some friends of ours from Clitheroe came over to see us and brought along their two Chihuahuas, which travelled in small carrying cases on the back seat of their car. Their little dogs soon made friends with our Chico. At the end of the day when it was time to go home, Chico was having a sniff round inside one of the boxes and was not noticed. He ended up in a strange box with a dog he had just met, having a ride in the back of a car towards Clitheroe! Luckily our friends stopped for a short break halfway and an unfamiliar face appeared when they looked into one of their dog boxes. They rang us and I set off to meet them and bring Chico home. He was such a character and we had him for seventeen years.

Times to remember

Wild weather

Grange-over-Sands is just a wonderful place to live. It is picturesquely situated in a sheltered position on the northern shores of Morecambe Bay, free from keen winds and fierce storms. That was until the night of 18th November 1977, which brought the worst gales and highest tides that I have ever seen while living at Guide's Farm.

Our neighbour and fisherman, Jack Burrow at Cart Lane crossing cottage, owned a large and heavy rowing boat and had taken it off the sands for the winter months. He had moored it well above high water mark on the stone ramp just over the railway crossing. The mooring rope was fastened to the railway wall and wrapped around one of the large coping stones, which should have been enough to have secured the Queen Mary. Yet when the tide came so high, the tremendous waves and gale force wind were continuously battering it against the crossing gate.

Eva Burrow, Jack's wife, came along to the farm about midnight. Olive and I had just gone upstairs to bed, so we were not asleep and soon got ourselves dressed and came downstairs to see who it was at the door. Eva was very worried and asked if I would go along and help, as she feared their boat would be smashed to pieces. I went along the lane with Eva and we could hear the storm at its full height. Huge waves were pounding the railway embankment and the spray from them was coming well over onto the line. When we arrived on the other side of the crossing I had never seen anything like it as each wave surged towards us through the gate and washed on to the railway.

We could see that this was going to be dangerous so we chose our time, opening the crossing gates

between the enormous waves. By a stroke of good luck we managed to grab the mooring rope and on the next wave pulled like mad at the boat. It came right up to the highest point on the level crossing near to the wall and that is where it stayed for a very long time.

Although the extremely high tides and gales did a tremendous amount of damage all round the Morecambe Bay coastline, it was Grange, Arnside and Sandside that took the brunt of the storm. The memories of that Friday night stayed with me for quite some time as my access onto the sands in those days was mainly over Cart Lane crossing. I used to pass by Jack Burrow's rowing boat and be reminded of that terrible night with one of the highest tides I had ever seen.

A load of hot air

During our forty years at the farm we have understandably met many people and made lots of new friends. On one of the most beautiful days in the summer of 1981 I arranged a walk from Hest Bank to Grange for the Cherry family, whom I had not previously met. The following March I received a letter from Peter, their 22-year old son, explaining that he wanted to write a book on Morecambe Bay and asking if it would it be possible to go out to the fishing grounds with me and take some photographs. Arrangements were duly made and Olive and I found that he was a very polite and well-educated young man, rather shy at first, but he seemed to come out of his shell with more frequent visits to see us. After a while it was like coming home for him and we always made him welcome.

It was very good of the Cherry family to include us in some of Peter's birthday celebrations, when we were taken out to the Lakeside and

Crooklands hotels and had wonderful meals. We did not always celebrate in such style, but many a time following a walk Olive and daughter Jean would prepare a superb buffet for us. If the weather was nice we could enjoy eating outdoors on the lawn with the wonderful views of the Bay.

One afternoon in July 1987 the Cherry family had been on the Bay walk with me and were invited back to Guide's Farm for their tea. We were all sitting enjoying the relaxation and had just started our meal when suddenly we heard an almighty roar above our heads. It was a hot air balloon that was descending fast, just missing the chimney stack on the roof of Guide's Farm. They were so low that we shouted to the three occupants and we could see that they were going to come down very soon. As we watched, the huge balloon hit the dry sand almost tipping out its passengers, then it appeared to lift for a while but came down again about a mile from the shore.

These balloon enthusiasts always have a back-up vehicle to come to their aid, but on this unfortunate landing it was unable to travel across the sands to reach them as it got bogged down in soft sand not far out from the shore at Kents Bank. Luckily for them, they had been spotted by us at the farm and I wasted no time in going out to their rescue as the tide was coming in and was not too far from where they had landed.

The balloon canopy had already been rolled up in a tidy heap and there were just enough of us to lift the heavy basket onto the backboard of my tractor. The tide was only a matter of yards away from us as we drove slowly back towards Kents Bank station, where I helped transfer the heavy basket onto the back-up vehicle's trailer. The balloon belonged to Holker Estates and was valued at £10,000 so they were very pleased to see us all back.

The balloon trip that nearly ended in disaster had been intended as a 63rd birthday treat for Alfred Shepherd of Barrow. He believed they were going to crash as there was no wind to keep them up

and as they came down they had in fact bounced three times on the sand before coming to a halt.

My good deed done for the day, I drove back to Guide's Farm to meet up with Olive, Jean, Chris and the Cherry family. I was able to finish my meal and discuss the rescue with them, although they had been able to watch what was happening quite clearly from the farm.

Last rites
Something totally different from anything I had been asked to do before was to carry out the wishes of three residents of Cart Lane. When they had died and been cremated, they wanted their ashes to be taken and scattered out in the Bay.

This I did on two occasions before the River Kent moved across to the other side of the Bay. Now it is just not the same, so with my most recent request I suggested that it would be better for me to travel round to Arnside and meet up with the family and their friends on the promenade. After these arrangements were settled, Olive and I set out from Grange with me looking smart and dressed like a funeral director. Olive did not take part in the service and sat patiently waiting in the car until it was all over.

I had earlier suggested what I thought would be the most suitable place, so after being introduced to the small party and having a brief chat, I asked them to follow me down onto the shore towards the edge of the Kent. Here we all stood solemnly and in silence. A member of the family was carrying a bunch of red roses and handed one to each of us, then took out a sheet of paper with some very nice wording that she read out.

The tide was just about to lap over our feet when I was given the urn containing the ashes. Now it was my turn. Nothing emerged with the first shake so I tried harder and you will rarely have seen what happened next. Well, if you pee into the wind you definitely get your own back! What had been a gentle breeze had become much stronger and I was covered in grey ash from head to toe - and so were some of the relatives. Nothing was said as we threw the roses onto the moving tide and then there was another reading from the sheet of paper.

When it was all over and I returned to the car, Olive asked what I had been doing as my dark suit had changed colour to grey. I explained about

the wind coming in with the tide as it does many a time, but some good came out of that day at Arnside. Olive now trims my hair and eyebrows almost weekly. She says she has never known anyone whose hair grows as quickly as mine does - and by the way my suit had to go to the cleaners!

Distinguished visitors

In November 1994 the living room at Guide's Farm was transformed into a recording studio! I have never seen so much equipment, but the programme was going out live as the last in a series of eight midweek outside broadcasts from around Britain. Libby Purves and guests gathered here at the farm. The guest interviewer was Bob Langley, who I had not seen since he rode across the Bay in a horse-drawn carriage. As described in Part 2 of this book, I was then on horseback as the Guide taking part in the film 'Lakeland Summer'.

It really was good to meet up with Bob again and introduce him to Olive who had been busy plying everyone with cups of tea. Bob's interview was with Jim Bowen, the star of 'Bullseye', who lived near us. It was then the turn of Sophie Thurnham, a Cumbrian travel writer. She went to Romania planning to spend a couple of months gathering material to write a book but ended up working in an orphanage and psychiatric institution and was unable to leave. Next in line was Sandy Cox from Lancashire who hunts vermin and cleans drains! Finally, Libby Purves interviewed me. The programme really was appreciated and received very good feedback.

Much more recently, I read a tribute in the Barrow Evening Mail to Wynn Langton, a lifelong campaigner for peace, justice and socialism, who died in March 2003, aged 93, at a nursing home in Aldingham. Olive and I became friends with Mrs Elsie Williams, a widow who lived at Kents Bank with her faithful companion, a rough collie rescue dog called Zie. Mrs Williams and Wynn were great friends who shared the same beliefs and often spent time together. This is how we came to know Wynn and on one occasion I took both of them for a ride on my tractor out in the Bay. They did enjoy this outing and took lots of photographs.

One day Elsie rang us to say that the Vietnamese ambassador would be visiting us at the farm that afternoon. I was absolutely flabbergasted as we were in the middle of plastering the staircase! Our son-in-law Chris had knocked all the old plaster off and there was dust everywhere. There was just no way that we could get straight for them in so little time. Poor Olive did her best to tidy up the living room and we just had to hope that they did not want to visit the bathroom as this was upstairs. Promptly at two o'clock a long black limousine drew up in front of Guide's Farm!

As the knocker sounded I opened the door wearing a pair of tattered, paint-spattered jeans and was introduced. The ambassador must have liked me because he immediately kissed me on both cheeks. Chris looked on, no doubt amused, although his jeans were falling apart with a broken fly zip held together with safety pins. Olive did not know what to say but the visitors understood and stayed for tea. They also managed to find their way up to the bathroom with Olive close behind, holding up the most beautiful dress worn by the ambassador's wife and trying to protect it from the sharp treads on every step of the wooden staircase.

Looking back, so many events that have taken place at Guide's Farm that we are both amazed at how we have been able to cope. In a way we would not have wanted it to be any different. I suppose it would have been nice to have had a break once in a while, as neither of us have had a holiday in the last fifty years or so, but we are happy and contended in what we do, which must mean something.

Special occasions

In 1989 I was awarded an honourary MSc fellowship at Lancashire Polytechnic, now the University of Central Lancashire, Preston, and in 1996 was given an honourary MSc at Lancaster University, both awards being in recognition of my services to the community. Olive and I are invited back to both universities on a regular basis, but with our busy life we cannot attend as often as we would like. However, we have managed to attend the award ceremonies at Central Lancashire University for the past fourteen years. We are given a choice of days and always look forward to this wonderful occasion and the hospitality given to us.

We also receive an invitation each year to attend the Honourary Fellows' Dinner at the university. Here we meet up with old and new friends. This is a very nice way of getting to know a little about the new Fellows as we have a drink and a chat before the award ceremonies. We also appreciate the very efficient and polite staff, who keep things running smoothly and to order. The meal is always outstanding.

I had guided walks for Dr Barnardos for a number of years and was well known by the organisers, so I was pleased and looking forward to this occasion when in May 1994 they invited me, together with a young Tracy Barlow from Coronation Street, to open their garden fete. There was plenty of sunshine with a really good attendance and I believe their 'big day' was most successful.

In 1998 I was voted 'Cumbria Personality of the Year' for services to tourism and was presented with the Bernard A Gooch Award by the Commercial Members Group of Cumbria Tourist Board. This event took place at the Shap Well's Hotel.

In July 1999 a service was held in the Priory Church at Lancaster in the presence of the Queen and the Duke of Edinburgh. I was invited but was rather disappointed that I could not take Olive along with me. As I took the train from Kents Bank station there were plenty of empty seats so I chose to sit where I could wave to her as we sped past Guide's Farm.

At Carnforth a well-dressed couple got onto the train and chose seats opposite me. The lady was wearing a most beautiful outfit in blue with a hat that was almost as big as a small umbrella. I thought to myself - I bet they are going to the same place as I am. We did not speak at all on the journey and at Lancaster station the couple left the train with me following close behind. I had not been to the Priory Church before so I kept hard on their heels. They broke the ice by speaking first and asked if I was going to the church service. I told them that I had also been invited to the Royal Luncheon in the Town Hall at which they seemed surprised and said that I must be one of the lucky ones.

After the service we travelled by coach to the Town Hall where the luncheon was held. My greatest surprise was to find that I would be sitting on Top Table 2, along with the Duke of Edinburgh and many other famous people. They included Mrs Joan Bartholemew, widow of the great comedian Eric Morecambe, whose statue had been unveiled by the Queen earlier in the day.

A really memorable day in more ways than one occurred later in 1999 when Olive and I were driven down to an investiture at Buckingham Palace where I was to receive the MBE from the Queen. I was so nervous but once I had met the

Queen and shaken her hand I began to feel more relaxed. As I stepped back two paces, giving a slight bow, my brand new braces flipped loose from my trousers, first on the right side and then the left. I was wearing a hired suit and the trousers were slightly big round my waist. I gripped them tightly with both hands and prayed they would stay up till I got back to Olive in the audience. They did.

In December 2000 we were both excited when we received an invitation from local artist Fiona Clucas to open her exhibition at the Brewery Arts Centre in Kendal. Another artist, Tony Roberts from Bentham, who went out with me into the heart of Morecambe Bay to take lots of photographs, invited both of us to open his art exhibition at Settle, which we again enjoyed.

In August 2001 I officially opened a sensory garden at Hazel Bank Nursing Home, Yanwath, near Penrith. I was asked to plant a tree to commemorate the event and a plaque with my name and the date of opening was inscribed and inserted into the wall of the building. In the grounds was a confectionery stall where the public had to guess the weight of a large cake. I was the lucky winner and the cake was a jolly good one that lasted us a long time!

Another enjoyable occasion was in April 2002 when Olive and I opened the new exhibition at Cartmel Gatehouse Heritage Centre. We arrived in period costume in a horse-drawn carriage to be greeted by a crowd of visitors and residents. We were welcomed as guests of honour by John Coward, chairman of Cartmel Village Society, and were then introduced to the exhibition's project leader, Christine Stringfellow. After the opening we all entered the medieval building through its ancient spiral staircase. This innovative exhibition is located on three floors and depicts the history of the gatehouse, the development of Cartmel village, and the geography and geology of the surrounding area.

I enjoy giving lectures, with Olive showing slides of my life and work on Morecambe Bay, and there have been some special occasions with delegates from afar. When the United Nations held a conference at the Headway Hotel in Morecambe overlooking the Bay, it was well attended by delegates from this country and overseas and I was invited as guest speaker. Another full house was at Lancaster University to groups from Areas of Outstanding National Beauty when I was again guest speaker.

I am a lover of brass bands and had no hesitation in accepting when Olive and I were invited to Preston Guild Hall by Kevin Lonegan, who works for the town's Blind Society and now Galloway's of Chorley. The occasion was a 'Last Night of the Proms' and the bands were BNFL and the GJB sports company. It was a really wonderful and entertaining evening that we did not want to end.

In March 2001 I was presented with a Civic Award 'in recognition and sincere appreciation for services rendered to the Community life and well being of the citizens of Grange-over-Sands'. The mayor, A. Pamela Monkhouse, and the town clerk, D. Whittington, signed it on behalf of the townspeople of Grange. I received the award at the Victoria Hall and was so moved to tears that I could barely respond.

At a meeting in the Coronation Hall, Ulverston, in September 2002 the Trustees of the Morecambe Bay Partnership awarded Olive and me Honourary Life Membership. They presented us with a framed certificate with wording as follows: 'In recognition of their tremendous work, the welcome they extend to so many people, their love of the Bay which they so gracefully and naturally share, and the respect they show for the Bay and all of us.'

We both feel so proud at being chosen for this wonderful award and shall treasure it forever.

Leading from the front

In 1993 I felt that my world had come to an end. I had a suspected heart attack and was taken to Furness General Hospital at Barrow by ambulance, where I was put in intensive care for about a week. When I eventually felt much better and was allowed home, I had to take things easy for a while. I became fit enough to go back onto the sands and lead the walks, but if the wind was strong I did so from my tractor. When the weather was mild I led the walkers on foot and by working this way I managed to build up my strength once again.

On 14th June the following year I came home from the sands after accompanying a small group of Americans. Olive met me at the yard gate. I shall never forget that day and how frightened I felt when she told me she had received a telephone call from Blackpool Victoria Hospital and I was to be admitted the very next day as there was a bed available. The operation for double by-pass open-heart surgery would take place the following day and my surgeon would be Mr Khan.

After surgery Olive phoned the hospital and they said she could ring the nurse every hour during the night until I was stable. I was in intensive care until the 19th when I was moved to Ward 10. Olive and our daughter Jean made the journey to Blackpool every day to see me. On 24th June it was thought that I was well enough to be sent home, so Olive arranged with our friend Christine to drive to the hospital and bring me back to Guide's Farm. The doctors, nurses and staff were just wonderful and when it was time for us to leave the hospital they came to see us off and say their goodbyes. They told me that I was not an invalid but should stick to a sensible diet. When I felt fit enough I was to get out there onto those sands and do what I did best - walking across the Bay and meeting up with all those lovely people.

I took their advice and have been back on my feet now for the past nine years doing just that, leading from the front and not riding on a tractor as many people think. As each new season approaches I still get that 'feel good' factor. Is it something in the air - or maybe the water? I can't tell you.

Appendix

Shall the guides be continued?

Extract from the Lancashire Guardian - May 3rd 1873

An enquiry was held on Friday at Grange Hotel by J.T. Fell Esq with the view of enquiring into the conduct of John Nevison, the Guide, and whether it is desirable that the office of Guide should still be maintained. Mr Jackson represented the Chancellor of the Duchy, Mr Poole represented J. S. Young Esq and Mr Tilly represented John Nevison the Guide.

Mr Fell explained that the enquiry was instituted, owing, he was informed, to certain serious offences having been committed by the present Guide which had been tried before the magistrates, and which had caused certain persons in the neighbourhood to inform the Chancellor of the Duchy that he was not a proper person to be trusted with the performance of duties so much affecting the public interest.

He then read a communication authorising him to hold an enquiry in such a manner as would enable him to advise the Chancellor of the Duchy, whether it was desirable to make any change, and if so, what the change should consist of.

The letter was accompanied by the following memorandum: The officer, commonly called the Guide over Kent Sands, but described by the patent of the existing Guide or 'Keeper, Conductor and Governor' of the sands near Cartmel, called Kent Sands, otherwise Kent Sands in the County Palatine of Lancaster, was anterior to the dissolution of the monasteries, appointed by the priors of Cartmel, who had certain revenues (including Peter's pence) allowed for the maintenance of a Guide stationed at the ford of the united streams of the Kent and the Winster.

In the 16th Century the revenues of the Priory of Cartmel became vested in the King in right of his Duchy of Lancaster, and since that time the Guide has been appointed by patent under the seals of the Duchy and County Palatine.

The earliest Duchy patent bears the date 29 January 1548 and grants to Thomas Hodgson the office of Guide with one tenement of land at Kents Bank and other liberties, advantages, easements, and profits to the same office of old time, due and accustomed, and also the fee and wages of £5 per annum to be received yearly out of the issues, profits and revenues of the lands, tenements, and other hereditaments and possessions whatsoever of the late priory of Cartmel.

The modern salary is expressed to be chargeable in the same way, although it does not appear that Her Majesty now derives any revenues from the dissolved priory, all the lands of which seem to have been granted in fee about the commencement of the 17th Century.

The fee of £5 continued to be paid to the guide until about 1780, when it seems to have been raised to £12, which was increased to the present fee of £32 under minute of the Duchy Court of 22nd July 1820, by which it was proposed that £10 part thereof was paid by the Guide to his assistant at the River Keer.

By the earliest of the existing patent, the Guide was required to repair the 'Carter's House' but in 1805 a sum of £100 was paid to William Carter, the then guide, to be expended in and towards the repairs of the dwellinghouse, appropriated for the residence of the said guide.

On the construction of the Ulverston and Lancaster (now Furness) Railway in 1860 a strip of land containing three roods and 15 poles was granted to the Company under the Duchy seal in consideration of the sum of £84 7s 6d, which was invested in consuls, the dividends from which have since been paid annually to the Guide during the tenure of his office.

John Nevison, the present guide, was appointed by patent dated 10th December 1867, on the recommendation of gentlemen in the neighbourhood, as the stepson of James Carter, the last guide and assistant. He was appointed during Her Majesty's pleasure.

The examination of witnesses was then proceeded with. None of the witnesses was sworn, but Mr Fell stated that if it was found in any case desirable to have a statutory declaration, they could have it so.

John Nevison, the guide, said:

I have been guide for a period of six years since last September. John Carter preceded in the office. My duty is to attend the sands when the tide is out. I usually go on the sands as soon as ever it is low water. I go on horseback. Since the period that I was appointed guide five or six persons have crossed the sands in a day sometime, and other days there are none. Most of them are foot passengers. They are generally on the way to Ulverston or Barrow, or back again.

The number of persons crossing is increasing. We have had more the last twelve months than we have had for a long time. Three or four horses and carts in the winter time but in summer we have a good many carriages.

The majority of persons come from Silverdale, or from Warton Lane Ends near Carnforth. Very few persons cross from Hest-Bank. I go out as far as the pier 'S/dale' sometimes once a week, sometimes once a fortnight when the crossing is

good. I have no assistant at the Keer, he was given up in Carter's time. When the channels are fordable, I am on the sands sometimes, whenever I know that there is someone coming. I go daily, or when I do not go I have a man that does. I have only a boy at present, his name is Pladdy, and he is about 16 years of age. The boy knows where the ford is. When I have not been there I have been sometimes at one place and sometimes at another.

I go to Ulverston Market sometimes once a week. The boy has been brought up as a farm servant. It is stated in my patent that I can have a deputy. This John Pladdy has lived with me since Martinmas. He lived before just above Grange here.

About a fortnight after he first became my servant he took people across and I was with him. There is a Market at Lancaster, once a week, and I might go there on a Saturday, and Ulverston on a Thursday perhaps. Sometimes when I went away perhaps I was selling apples, and sometimes pigs. I occupy properly in my office as Guide.

I have ten acres altogether, including my orchard. I am aware that complaints have been made that I have not fulfilled my duties. No complaints have been made to me.

During the period that I have been guide, one loss of life has occurred. It took place about two hours before low water. The person was crossing having come out from Arnside and right down towards Grange. I did not see it, but I saw him being brought out.

By Mr Poole:

On the 7th March I wrote to the Duchy and in the letter I stated that not one had been lost during any time of doing my duty.

At the time I wrote the letter I knew the man had been drowned, and I did not mention it, because it was not in my time of doing duty. I am bound to do duty only when the tide is out, and if anybody gets drowned at high water I can't help it. It is my duty to keep people off the sands when it is dangerous, if I can get to them.

For anything that I know the two convictions mentioned in the letter are the only two convictions mentioned against me. I do not know that I was convicted of drunkenness on the 5th of April 1872.

On the 15th August 1872 I was convicted for allowing my donkey and cart to stray on the high road. At that time I was at Newton-in-Cartmel in a public house, but I only had a glass of beer. My donkey left me about four miles. In October1869, I was not convicted of being drunk at Dalton that I know of. I was convicted at Ulverston for drunkenness at Dalton in that month.

On December 3rd 1872, I was fined £1 and costs for being drunk in the Magistrate's room. I was not disorderly, although I believe I did speak once. On the 30th June 1868, I was apprehended for a rape. I was put on trial and acquitted.

William Bell of Allithwaite was the man I had as deputy before the present boy. Sometimes he lived with me, and sometimes he went home. He is 50 years of age, and knows the sands. I am not aware that I am obliged to keep a cart for the conveyance of carts across the sands. I have known only one woman come across in a cart in my time, and she crossed in a fisherman's cart. The man was drowned just above the station here. I do not often go to Dickinson's public house at Allithwaite, and stay there for a whole day.

Policemen at Grange and Cartmel have not frequently complained of my drinking, although they have spoken to me about it. They have not complained of my furious driving, except on the occasion that I was fired.

I obtained the office of Guide on the recommendation of a certain gentleman, and it was not understood that I would only hold it until Mr Carter's son came of age.

By Mr Tilly:
It has never been suggested to me to resign on account of somebody else coming of age.

I was brought up with the late Mr Carter, the last guide. I have been acquainted with the sands ever since I was old enough to attend to business. For eight years before he died, I was allowed to take parties across. The railway stopped the coaches and the carriers' carts. When the coach was coming persons would know when it did come, and follow behind it, but now people come at any time, and that makes us look more after them.

Although the traffic is diminished, it is altered in its character. I always keep a horse. My duties require that I keep a horse. I gave £17 for the horse I have at present. I have to go to the channel every day to see if the ford has changed.

I have saved perhaps four or five persons who have been in danger and would have been drowned but for my assistance. Nobody has complained to me that they wanted a guide and could not find me. When I have gone to market I have not neglected my duties. The charge of rape was a false charge, and I was acquitted, the judge having stopped the case.

Most of the people who come across the sands now are poor people. The cocklers sometimes cockle at the other side of the channel, but I have nothing to do with them as they know what they are doing.

William Carter said:
I am brother of the late James Carter, and am living in Dalton. I work in the mines. I have known the sands all my life, in fact I was brought up in Cart Lane. I often helped my father when he was guide. It is now 25 years since I acted as guide to anybody. At that time there was a great deal of traffic and no railway.

The guide at that time always went onto the sands when there was a possibility of anybody crossing, five hours after the ebb. It was not considered part of his duties to remain there after sunset. He had a cart to be used if needed, but in short tides we did not often take a cart.

My father took a cart more than we did. My father paid £10 to the landlord of Hest Bank to act as a Keer Guide. It was usual to brob the sands in winter. The brobs were made of broom, and we used to repair them every fortnight. I think it is a good idea in bad weather to have the sands marked in that way. I know all the property connected with the guide, and it has been in our family for more than two hundred years. Nevison was then acting as guide. If the value of the land is not worth more than forty-five shillings it is much reduced. I have heard that Nevison only held the office until the coming of age of my brother's son.

John Nevison (recalled):
I do not know who appointed the Keer Guide. With regard to the channel on Lancaster sands, it is very awkward, and has never been so awkward since I came to it.

The sands are pretty good with the exception of the channel. I do nothing in the way of brobbing the sands in winter, except where I am crossing at. It has never been brobbed since the railway started, I believe. The rateable value of the guide's property is £42.

Mr John Hall:
The persons interested in crossing the sands - carriers, etc - subscribed something towards brobbing the sands. It was a voluntary subscription. I think brobbing to be very useful in winter time.

The money for brobbing was paid on the quantity of passes. It would be dangerous crossing the sands in misty weather when they were not brobbed. It would be a benefit to us, as well as those persons who passed. I do not think the sands have been brobbed since the formation of the railway.

J. S. Young Esq, Kents Bank:
The railway had just started when I came to Kents Bank. The traffic has greatly fallen off since the railway was finished. Kents Bank is very rarely used. I very rarely observe persons crossing the sands, or see the guide. I do not know the crossing, the guide may be there, but I do not see him. I do not look for him. Two men and a woman would have been drowned some years ago if I had not seen them and set them right. They came over from the Lancaster side. They were crossing at the wrong place, and with a good deal of signalling we got them to understand the right place to go over. I do not think the guide was there at all. I have seen people drowned, but I do not think that anybody was to blame. In my opinion it would certainly not be advisable to discontinue the guides. I have seen more foot passengers than carts crossing.

I also know the property occupied by the guide. Anything in the shape of land that Nevison has taken in hand is simply disgraceful. He has had some of mine and I am ashamed to own it.

Any respectable steady man could farm the land and attend to his duties as guide at the same time. I know my own knowledge of his previous conduct has been very unsatisfactory and very disorderly. He was sold up some time ago, and I thought it was such a scandal that I had better report him. The selling off was occasioned by his drunken conduct.

When Nevison was appointed I understood that he would resign the office when Carter's son was ready for it. If his previous conduct has been anything like decent, I do not think any man in the parish would speak a word against him. Such a man I consider is totally unfit for the office. He is well known as the most disorderly man in the parish.

By Mr Tilley:
I do not know that I can point out any particular instance when he neglected his duty as guide. I could not swear that the case of the two men and a woman took place in Nevison's time, and another case of an Irishman on tramp, I think did not occur in his time. Several accidents happened before Nevison's time but I can only say that one has taken place during the period that Nevison held office.

Thomas Rawlinson said:
I live at Cart Lane and have done so for thirty-four years, and have known Lancaster Sands all my life. When I first knew them there was a great

deal of crossings. The traffic began to fall off since the new railway began. James Carter the younger was guide then, I never heard of any complaints while he was guide. Since then, I have observed people crossing the sands. People generally come out at Cart Lane now, when they cross the sands. I think it would not be advisable to do without the guide. The guide has time to attend his duties and the land at the same time.

By Mr Tilley:
I never heard of any complaints that Nevison was not forthcoming when wanted.

Dr Beardsley said:
I have resided in Grange some years and have frequently observed people crossing the sands. It has occurred to me to cross the sands when I required to go to Silverdale on business. I have gone both with and without a guide. When I went without I made enquiries about the fording place. When I wanted the guide, he was there. In summertime it would be possible to come without the guide.

In my opinion it is a matter of public importance that the office of guide should be maintained.

Mr Westwood said:
I have been here for about eight years. A good many people still cross the sands. I have driven excursions and on such occasions I have let the guide know the day before.

When I have given notice to the guide he has always been in attendance. In my opinion it is very necessary that the office of guide should be maintained. Nevison has always attended to his duties when I conceived it necessary. I never heard anyone complain that he was not there when they wanted to cross.

George Sedgwick, labourer, Cart Lane, said that Nevison took beer sometimes but he had always found him perfectly fit for duty whenever he required his services.

David Orr said that he frequently drove people across the ford on pleasure and he had never had any difficulty with the guide, who either was there or sent his man. It is necessary that a steady man should hold it. There is no notice board at Grange as to persons going on to the sands, or that there is a guide at Cart Lane that I am aware of. I do not know that there is a notice board at Kents Bank, Silverdale, Warton or Hest Bank. In my opinion there should be instructions as to where the guide lives.

William Carter stated that there was a notice board on the house at Hest Bank, where the river Keer guide formerly lived.

Police Sergeant Holden said that on the 5th April, 1870 Nevison was fined for allowing his donkey to stray, and in December 1872 he was fined for being drunk. He had seen him once or twice in Cartmel under the influence of drink.

P.C. at Cartmel knew nothing of the kind beyond him drinking at times. He had seen him under the influence of drink on other occasions than those on the sands, and he then appeared quite fit to perform his duties. He thought the office a very desirable one.

Dr Hall gave it as to his opinion that the guide was still necessary.

After some further enquiry the proceedings closed. The minutes of the proceedings were sent to the Chancellor of the Duchy.

Great Books from

G R E A T   N O R T H E R N

The Great Yorkshire Celebrity Cookbook

Hannah Hauxwell: The Common-sense Book of a Countrywoman

The Two Way Guide to the Settle Line

The Tale of the Mouse

The Yorkshire Dales: A Landscape Through Time

Austin Mitchell's YORKSHIRE JOKES

Austin Mitchell's TALKIN' YORKSHER

The Wensleydale Railway

Richard Whiteley's YORKSHIRE QUIZ

Arthur Ransome and the World of the Swallows & Amazons

Sandwalker

Sand-pilot of Morecambe Bay

Come Down to the Wood

The Golden Age of the Yorkshire Seaside

Favourite Jokes: Share a Laugh with 100 Celebrities

**For further information on these or forthcoming titles
please call Great Northern Books on 01943 604027.**